W9-DAI-936

PLAYS
& HOW TO PUT THEM ON

By Moyne Rice Smith

PLAYS

& HOW TO PUT THEM ON

Illustrated by Don Bolognese

New York   1961

Henry Z. Walck, Incorporated

To the Princeton Junior Community Players

with deep gratitude to
Deborah and Blackie

CONTENTS

Have you ever wanted to put on a play, and not known how to go about it?

This book will tell you how to take a story idea and make it grow into the kind of play which fits your number of actors, your amount of time, your equipment and your acting spot. It will tell you about the things you will need if, after you've sampled the fun of playmaking and play acting, you want to continue to produce plays. It will then show you some plays which one group of children created, and explain how this group answered its "how do we do it" questions.

This book may help you find the right answers to your own particular questions about playmaking. As you read it, perhaps you will say, "Oh, that gives me an *idea!*"

STAGE TERMS

A few definitions to make you be efficient and sound professional.

Directions—always given from the actor's point of view as he stands on the stage facing the audience:

STAGE RIGHT—toward the actor's right hand

STAGE LEFT—toward the actor's left hand

STAGE CENTER—the middle of the stage

DOWNSTAGE—toward the front of the stage

UPSTAGE—toward the back of the stage

OFF STAGE or BACKSTAGE—the places at the sides or the back of the scenery not seen by the audience. Thus, off-stage right and off-stage left are the sides away from the actor's right and left

Properties or *Props*—everything used in the play except scenery and costumes:

HAND PROPS—small properties handled by actors

STAGE PROPS—the big furnishings of the play

Scenery terms:

BACKDROP—a drape or canvas at the back of the set

BORDER—a narrow drape across the top of the stage to hide the ceiling area

CURTAIN, FRONT CURTAIN or HOUSE CURTAIN—the curtain which separates the stage from the audience

CYCLORAMA or CYC—a large background curtain or canvas

PROSCENIUM ARCH—the front frame of the stage

SET—the stage set up to be a certain place

WINGS—spaces used for entrances and exits at the sides of the stage off the set

Lighting terms:

BORDER LIGHTS—sections of lights hung above the stage

FLOODLIGHTS—lights which can be focused on large areas

FOOTLIGHTS—strips of lights on the floor at the downstage edge of the stage

GELATINS—colored sheets of gelatin placed over bulbs to give colored light

HOUSE LIGHTS—the lights in the audience's part of the building

SPOTLIGHTS—lights which can be focused on small areas

SWITCHBOARD or LIGHT BOARD—a panel of light switches off stage

General terms:

CUE

for an actor—the lines which come immediately before his own actions or speeches

for a backstage worker—the lines which come immediately before a change in lights, or a sound effect, or a "curtain," etc.

BLOCKING—working out positions and movements of the actors

"CURTAIN"—the signal that opens or closes a scene

CURTAIN CALL—the bow taken by the actors after the play is over

CLEAR—to clear the stage of actors, scenery and props in order to set the stage for the next scene

PANTOMIME—action without speech

"PLACES"—the signal for everyone, off stage and on, to be in his proper place to start a scene

RUN-THROUGH—a rehearsal of the whole play which does not stop to practice special sections

SCRIPT—a copy of the play

STRIKE—to take down a scene from the stage (to strike a set)

CHOOSING YOUR STORY

Start with a story you like. This may be one you make up, or one which another storyteller has made up. There are many wonderful stories from which to choose: legends, myths, Bible stories, folk tales, fairy stories, hero adventures, jungle, Indian, pioneer, animal, circus stories. You may want to choose one to fit the time of year or a particular holiday. There are many plays to be made about the different seasons, and about Halloween, Thanksgiving, Christmas, New Year's Day, Valentine's Day, Easter, the Fourth of July and famous birthdays. Perhaps you will think of a story which would be good because of a special interest of your group or your school, church or community. But whatever story you choose, be sure that it is one which you all like and which you all think would be great fun to play-act.

The best stories for playmaking are the ones which make you ask "what happens next?" Remember when you were little and were listening to a good story, how you always wanted to know "and then what happens?" and could not bear to be told "we'll finish it another time"? This is the way the audience at your play should feel.

PLANNING YOUR PLAY

Study your story to see the plan of what happens in it. Can you act out this plan so it will be clear and interesting? You may have to take out parts of the story which seem to sidetrack it, or are too complicated for you to show properly. You will have to know what your play means from the beginning to the end. If you don't know, you can't show others.

Your playing space is your stage. It may be the end of an attic, playroom, garage, barn, schoolroom or auditorium, or a real ready-built theater. It may be a front yard, or a playground at school, or a piece of the park, or a meadow at camp, or a clearing under the apple tree.

The scene of your play is the place where the story happens. Scenery shows the audience what the place is supposed to be.

The playing space you have may even help you choose your story and the play that grows from it. This is particularly true if you are going to do a play outdoors, where your scenery is already made, waiting for the play which fits it.

A campfire circle would make a fine scene for a play about gypsies or Indians, or about witches making their magic brews. And it would be a perfect place for a pioneer play. Your actors might even come in a covered wagon pulled by a team of farm horses!

What better scenery could you want for elves or fairies than a ferny spot in the woods or garden on a dewy morning when sunbeams slant and birds twitter?

An outside stairway on your schoolhouse or apartment building is ready-made for a play about a princess imprisoned in a tower, or for Jack and the Beanstalk.

A park, playground or meadow is the right place for stories which need room for lots of action. It is exciting for an audience to see, from a distance, a group of knights coming with banners and trumpets, a procession of the Royal Court led by high-stepping guards, villagers bringing their carts and baskets to the market square, circus performers parading; or a single actor who, as he comes closer, is recognized by the audience as the Pied Piper, Wandering Minstrel or Horrible Headsman.

If your story happens in more than one place, you can change your outdoor scene by actually moving your audience to another place. Have a fairy cast a spell on the audience and lead them from a scene in the magic woods to the edge of the lake where the mermaids are swimming. Have a herald command the audience to follow him from the courtyard of the King to a battlefield. Have a Knight lead the audience from a tournament field to the tower where his Lady is awaiting rescue. Have a Pied Piper pipe the audience from the village square to the hillside.

The simplest way to have more than one scene is to tell the audience what the place is through action, rather than scenery. An audience will believe they are seeing a battlefield if soldiers are fighting there, even though a moment before they have believed it to be a castle garden because that was where the Princess and her Ladies were promenading. If you have carefully worked out in your dialogue and action the things you want the audience to believe, you will discover how much pretending the audience will do without even knowing that they are helping.

In an indoor play, a single piece of scenery can show what the scene is. You may decide to paint a mural on brown paper for a background to your play. A map which has on it the Eiffel Tower or the Arc de Triomphe means you are in Paris. The Empire State Building or the Wall Street skyline means New York. You will be in a cathedral if you have a stained-glass window, made of cardboard and colored paper; in a garden if there is a fence with vines and flowers; in a palace if there is a throne.

If your story happens in all three of these places, but the biggest action is in the garden, put the fence across the back of your stage, the cathedral window at one end of the stage, and the throne at the other. Then you can change your scene without closing a curtain to change scenery. To make these places seem farther apart, have your actors go through the audience, singing and talking as they journey from one scene to another. Or they might pretend to walk forward by marching in place, getting more and more out of breath as they talk of the difficulty of their long and hazardous adventure.

Another good way to have different scenes is to use your main stage for the big part of a play and a smaller stage for another scene. If you want to have a Prince find a child who is lost in the forest, put the forest scene on a separate little platform. Have the Prince gallop around the audience, to music, to reach the forest.

If most of your story takes place in a village square, but there is one part of it in which the mayor of the town goes to seek advice from an old woman who lives over-the-river-and-under-the-hill, you might have only one scene by letting the old woman come to the mayor in the village square; or you might have the mayor tell the other villagers what happened when he comes back from visiting the old woman, and not show the scene with her at all.

If you want to put different pieces of scenery or furniture on your stage while your play is going on, actors can bring these things on as part of the play. Your villagers can carry stools onto the stage when they come to the town meeting. A servant, guard or herald can move things on the stage as part of the performance of his character in the play. In Chinese plays, there is an actor called the property man, who stays on stage throughout the play to move and arrange things.

To change the time in your play is as simple as changing the place. If you are indoors, the easiest way is to turn out the lights and then turn them on again. Another way is to start each scene by having someone off stage strike a gong the right number of hours. A herald might carry a banner which says what day or month or year it is; or he might carry an enormous book and turn a page with a chapter title on it for each change in time and place. The right music will tell the audience that "now we are in a different part of the forest," or "now it is a different time in the story."

Another easy way to tell the audience what you want them to know is to have a narrator explain things. A nursemaid or a grandmother might start telling a story to some children, and then the play could become the story she is telling. An Oriental Potentate might begin with "This, O Best Beloved, is a story of Far-Off Times. . . ." A minstrel could tell part of a medieval play, as he sing-talks to his lute. Such a narrator, who of course is acting a part, can then continue his story whenever it seems wise to tell the audience something which is not being said by the actors themselves. The use of several narrators talking as a chorus is an especially good way to do a play outdoors, where the sound of an actor's voice may be lost in the wind, but the sound of a speaking group can be heard. But be careful, if you decide to use a narrator. It may mean you haven't tried hard enough to make the action tell the story.

You will think of other ways to change place and time which do not break the spell of telling the audience what happens next.

ORGANIZING YOUR PRODUCTION

After you have planned your play and know where you are going to give it, you will think of many questions about its production. Who will play the parts of the characters? How will you manage the rehearsals? Will you need to make some scenery? Do you need lighting? What will your actors wear? Will they need make-up? What will you need to furnish your stage? What things will your actors need to handle in the play? Do you need music or off-stage noises? Who will your audience be? How will you tell them about the play? Do they need tickets? What about a program? Who will show the audience where to sit? What will they sit on?

In order to start working out the answers to these questions in an orderly and efficient way, you will certainly need a general manager. He may be chosen from your group, or he may be an adult. He will be your director. He will guide your rehearsals and will be in charge of any committees you may wish to form.

A play, like every exciting and good thing, is made up of many separate ingredients. Without its particular ingredients put together in its special way, you would not have the thing itself. But it is the thing whole which is the wonder. It is when all the ingredients of a play—the characters, dialogue, action, scenery, costumes, sound effects, lights—lose their separateness that the play itself becomes a living, exciting experience. Your director will help you put all your ingredients together in the right proportions. While each of you is doing his own special job on stage or off, your director will be thinking of the play as a whole.

You may decide to have a scenery committee, a lighting committee, a costume committee, which might also be in charge of make-up, and a committee to take care of the things you need for your play which are neither scenery nor costumes. This is called a property committee. Stage properties, or props, are the things which furnish the stage; hand props are the things actors need to handle in the play. Your property committee might also be in charge of your off-stage music and sound effects.

An audience or house committee might take care of all the things which have to do with the audience. After you have decided who your audience is to be, this committee may want to write invitations, or make announcements, or advertise your play with posters, or write some stories about it for your camp or school or town newspaper, or put notices on bulletin boards, or even plan a parade about it. If you decide to have tickets, this committee can make them by hand, or type them, or have them printed. It will also get and place pillows, stools or chairs for the audience, have someone greet the audience, take their tickets, and help seat them. It may wish to make programs which tell the name of the play and the name of the author who wrote the story from which the play was made, the characters in the play and which of you are acting them, where and when the play takes place, and perhaps the names of your committee workers. Programs should also acknowledge any friends who have been particularly helpful to you in the production of your play and should thank the copyright owners of the story, if you have used a story for which permission has been necessary. You can determine whether you need to ask permission by looking in the front of the book or story you use to see whether there is a copyright notice. Publishers and authors are usually willing to let you use stories to make plays for your own delight when no admission is charged. You do not need to ask permission to use fairy tales, folk tales, legends, Bible stories and stories from the classics.

Some of you may choose to be on a committee and not act in the play. But if all of you want to act, you can use all the actors who want to be in the play by adding characters to those in the story. One interesting and easy way to use many actors is to have groups of people act and speak together. Often you can use any number of heralds, court ladies, court gentlemen, goblins, soldiers, animals, wisemen, villagers or witches. They will have fun working out a pattern and style of group action and speech. If you plan to give more than one performance of your play, you might have two casts, with actors taking turns in playing the parts. In rehearsing, both groups can be working at the same time if you have separate rooms, or the groups can alternate. Such double-casting helps, too, when an actor is absent; you will have a ready substitute.

There will be times in rehearsals when you are not on the stage and can be busy working on another part of the production. Playmaking is fun all the time if everyone is always busy. There are so many things to be done that there should never be a moment during rehearsals when anyone is just waiting to act.

REHEARSING YOUR PLAY

When you have thought through your story and have decided how you are going to try to show its meaning in action, you are ready to start your rehearsals. The first ones should be completely experimental, to see if your plan is a good one and to determine who your characters will be and what they will say. Try acting out your play according to your plan, just making it up as you go along.

You will already be well acquainted with the way the people in the story talk. There are many good ways to put an idea into conversation. Try different ways to see which one gets your play started best. For instance, a story which starts with "Once upon a time a King was very sad because his daughter never laughed" could, in the play, begin with the King asking his lovely Princess why she is always so sad; or the Court Ladies gossiping about the unfortunate state of affairs; or a group of hopeful suitors boasting to each other about what each will do to make the Princess laugh; or the King consulting his Wisemen about his problem; or the Princess seeking help from her Fairy Godmother. All good stories make you interested at the very beginning, so you must be sure to get your play off to a good start.

Since you know your story well, and know the sequence of its action, you will be able to make up your conversation by keeping the meaning of the story in mind as you talk to each other. There are two parts to conversation, speakers and listeners. Both are equally important. If you know what your story means and really listen to what another actor is saying, you will find that you can answer him without difficulty, and the dialogue will move along interestingly and naturally. Sometimes it is a good idea to try a part of a scene by acting it without words. This is called pantomime. It will make the action very clear to you, and then you will find it easier to put the right words with the action.

After you have acted out your story several times, and each one of you has tried any part he wants to, you will be ready to decide who will play each of the characters. This is called casting the play. A good way to do this is to have each actor tell what parts he would most like to do, and then have your group vote, on paper, for the casting which will make the best play. By now you will probably have had some surprises. Maybe one of you who is naturally quiet has, on stage, become the most rowdy of Giants. Perhaps someone who has always seemed shy has become the most haughty Queen. Perhaps the boy who is the funniest in real life has made the most mournful, droopy old Hermit. Maybe the prettiest girl has been the best crackly-voiced, scowling Witch. One of the most exciting things about acting is the way people turn into characters who are so different from their real-life selves.

You will find that after you have acted out your play several times you may know the play well enough so that you do not need to have it written down to learn. But if you want to have scripts, type them and clip them to cardboards. Shirt cardboards from the laundry are the right size, easy to handle, strong and convenient. Every actor should have the complete script and not just his own "lines." There are no lines in a play that mean anything when they stand alone. They make sense only because of what has gone before and what comes after, and how they relate to the story and to the other characters. You should all know the complete play. You will not be worried, then, if you need to take someone else's part.

Now you are ready to begin more formal rehearsals, in which you work out stage movements, groupings and characterizations so that they become constantly better.

Mark out your playing space so that you know where the entrances are. Set up boxes or chairs in the right places for your stage props. Have each actor use hand props from the first rehearsals. A piece of paper can be a substitute for a letter, or a stick for a gun; but they should be used from the beginning, so that they can help actors build their action and characterizations. A Knight must know how to carry his sword and where it is when he stands, walks, sits, kneels and fights. A Court Lady must know which hand her fan should be in when she lifts her long skirt at the Ball. Use pieces of costumes. You will become your character so much more quickly and easily if from the first rehearsals you wear a long train or a peaked hat or a robe or a long beard, and the right kind of shoes. If you are a member of Robin Hood's band, it should seem just as natural to you to wear tights as it does for you, as your own self, to wear shorts or dungarees. These clothes were not "costumes" to the people who really wore them.

You should begin each rehearsal by talking about the meaning of the play and deciding what you want to accomplish that day. Leave time enough at the end of the rehearsal to talk about whether you have done what you planned to do.

Often, instead of rehearsing your play from beginning to end, it is a good idea to start a rehearsal with a part of your play in which all of your actors are on the stage together, and work on this large-action scene while everyone is fresh. Or start with a scene which, for some reason, was difficult in the previous rehearsal. Problems which seemed unsolvable often become amusingly simple if they are tackled when everyone is rested. Sometimes one of you may come with an exciting new thought about some part of the play, and you may decide to experiment on this idea for an entire rehearsal period. A play is never finished until after the performance. As you rehearse, you will get more and more good ideas about how to make your play better. Each rehearsal should be creative, and not just a repeat of the last one.

In your rehearsals you will each be getting better acquainted with the character you are playing. You need to know all about him: what he looks like; how he laughs, walks, talks; where he lives; what he thinks, likes, and dislikes; who his friends and relatives are. Everything you think or do or say on the stage is a part of his character. If you are wondering whether another actor is going to make his entrance or say his lines at the right time, or whether the clock will strike, or the curtain will pull, then you are not "in character." You are worrying about things which the director is there to take care of. A Guard who stands up straight and listens, even though he has little to say, is "in character." If he slumps, or fidgets with his helmet, or wiggles his spear, he breaks the spell of "let's pretend" for everyone. Each actor must stretch his imagination in each rehearsal, so that it seems as if the story is happening that very minute. A good director will know when the actors lose the right feeling, and then you should stop for a rest. Have a cookie-break. Give your energy and imagination a chance to spring back to top form.

When you are ready to try to put together all the ingredients of your play, you will have your first dress rehearsal. This should be a very exciting time, but it should not be a trouble-

some time if you have rehearsed with substitute props and costumes, and have learned long before where everyone—on stage
and off—is supposed to be, and what he is doing, at all times
in the play.

This first dress rehearsal is a trial performance. The scenery
is in place, the lights are set properly, the actors are in costume
and make-up and know where their hand props are. Each person knows what his job is and when he will do it. The scenery
changers, the curtain puller, the electricians, the noisemakers
are ready. Each actor knows where he is to be off stage before
each entrance and after each exit. If he has to change his costume, he knows where he will do that. If there is an announcer,
he is at his place of entrance.

When all the actors and all the committees have reported
that they are ready, your director will start the rehearsal. No
matter what may go wrong, keep the story going and handle
every situation as you would if you were really the people in the
story instead of actors pretending. If you drop your fan, pick it
up as if you really are a Queen who drops her fan; or ask your
Maid to pick it up for you, and let her pick it up as a Queen's
Maid *would* pick it up. The director should make notes about
everything that needs to be fixed. After the rehearsal, talk
about how to fix things, so that they will be exactly right for the
next rehearsal.

At this first dress rehearsal, do not worry if everything does
not go smoothly, even though your planning has been fine.
You will find now that a mustache needs more glue, a hat needs
an elastic to keep it secure, a robe needs to be shortened, the
procession needs a little more music, a tree needs better bracing.

There should always be one or even two dress rehearsals before the final one. For the last dress rehearsal should be just the
way the performance is going to be, so you will all feel good
about everything.

But the last dress rehearsal, fine as it should be, will *not* be
just the way the performance is. Because some magic happens
at the performance. This magic happens because your play now

has added to it a final ingredient, the audience. The audience becomes a part of the experience in a way that is hard to explain, but in a way which you will all understand when you have closed your real or imaginary curtain on your first real performance.

THEATER EQUIPMENT

After you have experimented with playmaking and play acting, you may decide to have a group which continues to produce plays. If so, you will need some basic equipment for your theater. For some of the jobs, you will probably need to ask adult help.

STAGE

If you want to build a stage, the best kind is one which is made of plywood platforms the same height but of different widths and lengths. If you need to put your platforms away, make them so that each one will fit inside another for easy storage. The biggest one should be not more than 8 feet by 4 feet. 18 inches is a good height. Make them just like boxes. Put short slits in the sides for handholds, so you can easily move and lift them. Then you can combine your platforms to suit any play. You can have a big flat stage, a U- or L- or T-shaped stage, or a small stage separated from a larger one. Small platforms on top of bigger ones make good balconies and towers. Small platforms are also useful for thrones, benches, beds, seats and tables (Figure 1).

Make several sections of movable steps which can stand against your platforms. Actors can enter the stage by these steps, and can stand, sit or kneel on them in their stage action. On stage, a section of steps can be an entrance to a cathedral, or

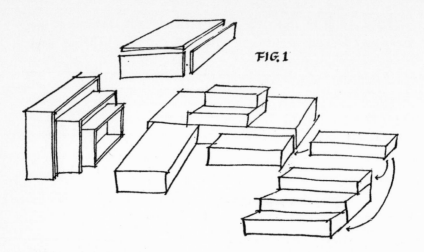

FIG. 1

the base of a high throne; or they can be covered with green drapes for mossy slopes.

If the roof of your room is very high, and if it has rafters or beams, you can make a false ceiling for your stage area. A good thing to use is a big heavy piece of coarse netting, the kind you can get from an army supply store. Attach this netting to a light frame and hang the frame from the rafters or beams. This fake ceiling will then be the top of your playing space. You can hang from it cutout birds, butterflies, insects and twisty vines to flutter above a jungle or garden; stars and fireflies to glitter in a fairyland night; paper lanterns to sway in a Chinese courtyard; cardboard chandeliers to light a ballroom or palace (Figure 2).

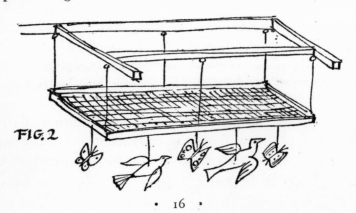

FIG. 2

If you want to cover the back wall of your stage area, one good way is to drape it. Use any material which hangs well. Strips of unbleached muslin or cotton flannel or monk's cloth stitched together and dyed soft blue make a good background drape. A government nylon parachute, which can be bought at an army surplus store, makes a beautiful backdrop. It opens up into an enormous lightweight circle of filmy white. Dye it

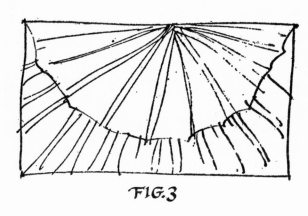

FIG.3

in a tub of sky-blue water paint. Cut it in half, and fasten the straight edge of one of the big half-circles to the top of your back wall. Then cut the other big half-circle in two, and hang these quarter sections at either side of the big one, spreading the folds to fan out at the bottom. It will look rather like an airy, giant cobweb (Figure 3).

To have a complete drape set, add to the big background drape narrow drapes at each side of the stage opening and half-way back on each side; and hang a strip drape as a border across the front of the top of your playing space. Be sure they are made of material thick enough that light will not show through them (Figure 4).

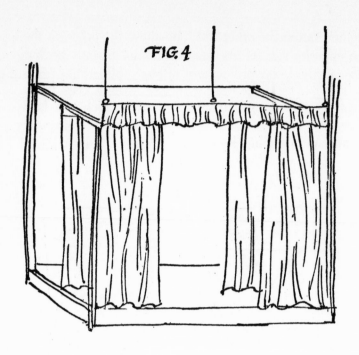

FIG. 4

Or, instead of using side drapes, you might place several tall trees at each end of your stage to hide the off-stage areas and to create good entrances. To make sturdy trees, nail lightweight beaverboard to long, narrow frames made of strips of 1″ x 3″ wood. Make beaverboard branches and clusters of leaves, and nail these to the tree frames with strips of wood backing. Paint the trees, and attach triangular wooden frames to the backs of them to brace them (Figure 5).

If you want to make front draw curtains which pull from one side of the stage, you need two curtains of heavy material attached to large curtain rings; four pulleys; and a clothesline rope twice as long as the width, plus twice the height, of your stage. Fasten one pulley at the top of one side of the stage opening and fasten the other two, one above the other, at the top of the opposite side of the stage opening. String the long rope through the lower pulley, and through the curtain rings of one

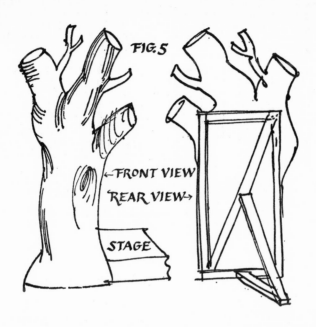

FIG. 5

←FRONT VIEW

REAR VIEW→

STAGE

curtain; then string the rope around the pulley on the opposite side of the stage and return the rope through the curtain rings of the other curtain, and over the top of the top pulley. The length of rope equal to twice the height of your curtain should then be brought through the fourth pulley and that pulley firmly fixed to the floor. When the curtains are hanging with an overlap in the middle, fasten each center ring firmly to its rope. By pulling the top rope, you can open the curtains; close them by pulling the lower rope. Arrange the rope so that the ends are tied together at the center of the closed curtains, so that the knot does not pass through any pulley. To make a good job of it, the whole structure needs to be supported by a pipe or a very taut wire, as shown in the diagram (Figure 6).

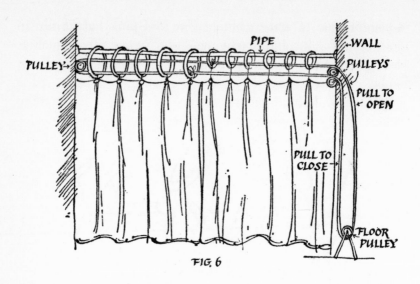

FIG. 6

Lighting

There are easy ways for you to light your stage even if you don't know a lot of complicated things about electricity. For general visibility, put lights behind your front border. Large "sealed-beam" lights are the best because they have jointed connections to their sockets and can be angled different ways to cut out unwanted shadows (Figure 7).

Experiment with lighting to get special effects for your plays. For side lighting, you can use ordinary floor or table lamps with foil reflectors.

You can make floodlights by lining wooden boxes with aluminum foil, boring holes in the boxes for the wiring, screwing base-socket receptacles in the boxes, and attaching extension cords to them (Figure 8).

Big flashlights make good spotlights to light small areas of the stage.

Natural light is made up of all colors, so you should not use white light only. You can get the effect of natural light by using a combination of amber, blue, white and pink light bulbs in your border lights and floodlights. For a special effect, such as sunlight through a window, cover a floodlight frame with an amber gelatin; for moonlight, a blue gelatin; for ghostly cold, a green gelatin. You can buy nonflammable gelatin sheets in many colors at a camera-supply store.

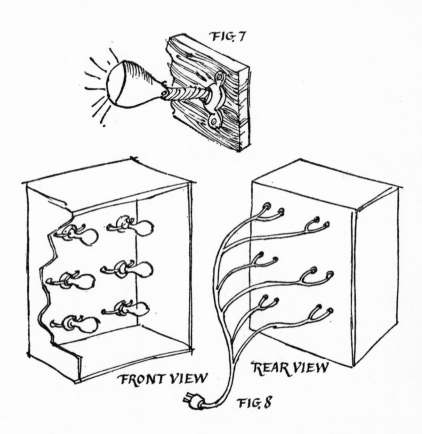

FIG. 7

FRONT VIEW   REAR VIEW

FIG. 8

Scenery

Lightweight screens which stand without bracing make the simplest and most practical scenery. You can make them by nailing wallboard or unbleached muslin on both sides of wooden frames six feet high by four feet wide. On each screen put double-action hinges with removable pins, so that all the screens can be hinged to stand together or to stand in however many sections you choose (Figure 9). Six of these screens, painted on both sides, will provide many different combinations of scenery. You can paint and repaint them with water paint for your different plays. If you cover your screens with cloth, you will need to put a first coat of "sizing" paint on them before you paint them as scenery.

Smaller screens, made the same way and painted like rock walls, are very useful (Figure 10).

You may wish to have a latticed six-foot-high, two-section window which can be angled to stand alone or can be hinged between sections of your tall screens. You can twine vines through it, fill it with colored-paper panes, or drape it with curtains.

The most useful building materials for your scenery are 1″ x

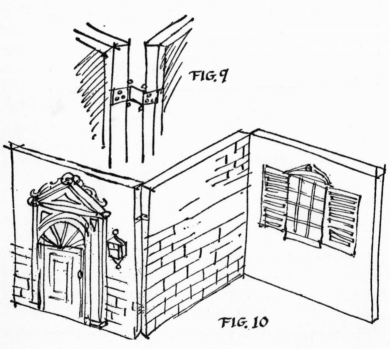

FIG. 9

FIG. 10

3", 1" x 2", 2" x 3" strips of soft pine; thin pressed-wood building board; plywood; beaverboard; cardboard; canvas; chicken wire. Have a place for the spares and odds and ends of all these materials, for you will constantly be wanting a little piece of one of them.

Have a big box for your tools, and take good care of all that you can beg, borrow or buy. As in any workshop, you will need hammers, saws and pliers. Wire clippers, pulleys and staplers are also very useful. Label small jars or boxes for each kind of nail, screw, tack, tape, chalk, pin, hook, hinge, string, wire.

In your paint supply you will need buckets, tin cans, newspapers, rags (lots of these, for they must not be kept after they become paint-daubed fire hazards), brushes, paint rollers, sponges, tape measures, charcoal, radiator paint, glitter spray, crayons and water paints. Water paints that you mix with cold water come in powder form in small quantities and wonderful colors. They easily wash off the scenery and you.

PROPERTIES

You will be able to borrow many of the properties which you need in your plays. Be sure that you take good care of anything you borrow, and return it immediately after your performance.

See how many of your props you can make. Paint, drape or nail cardboard cutouts to benches and boxes to make excellent beds, seats, tables, bushes, thrones, rocks. Make little houses, cages, hedges, counters and booths out of cardboard boxes. Make a stepladder into a tent, church or cave entrance (Figure 11).

Make your swords, trumpets, scrolls, banners, musical instruments sturdy enough so that they can be re-used or re-modeled for many plays.

A little wooden platform on roller-skate wheels is a handy thing to have to make things seem to move across the stage by themselves. This is called a "dolly." Fasten whatever prop you want on it, and pull it from off stage by an attached wire.

For sound effects have a big piece of tin to shake for thunder;

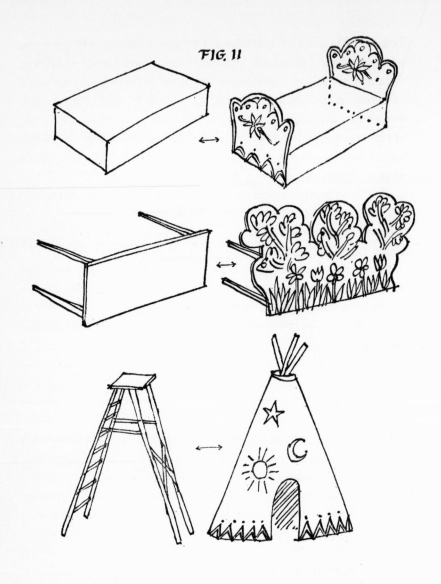

FIG. 11

a box of dried beans to rattle for rain; big pieces of sandpaper to rub together for surf; and any bells, drums, tambourines, whistles, gongs and Halloween noisemakers which you can collect. You can borrow a record player; but it is, of course, better to have one of your own. Perhaps someone will give you an old electric fan which you can keep to use for wind effects.

Materials which are especially useful in making hand props are chicken wire, old broom and mop handles, chair rungs, cardboard, corrugated paper, construction paper, crepe paper, foil, wrapping paper and paper bags. Good trimming materials which can be stapled or glued for decorative effects include beads, glitter, tinsel, fancy buttons, braid, fringe.

As your prop collection grows, you will need a well-organized prop corner or room in which to store your treasures.

COSTUMES

After you have finished your first play, and have returned promptly any costumes you have borrowed, you may have some costumes which you have made or which have been given to you. These costumes are the beginning of your own costume collection.

You will need a place to keep them. It should be a place big enough for your collection to grow. Of course, the best place is a room which is for costumes only. But you can use a corner of a room, or a closet.

The best way to set it up is to have a bar or rod high enough so that you can hang on hangers all of your floor-length costumes, such as evening dresses, robes and long capes. Have a lower bar for costumes like jackets, short dresses and smocks. Fasten skirts and pants to hangers with safety pins or clip clothespins.

Things which you do not hang should be put in boxes labeled clearly for contents. This arrangement will start your costume corner with a neat and efficient plan. Whenever anything is added, it should go into its proper place; whenever anything is used, it should be returned in good condition to its proper place. You may find, as your collection grows, that you need to subdivide your boxes. For instance, if you have started with only a few hats and have put them all into one box, later as you acquire more hats you may need to have separate boxes for different types of hats. A box which has started as "trimmings" may turn into several boxes of different kinds of trimmings: "braid," "lace," "feathers," "tinsel," "fancy buttons and beads," etc. If you follow this method, your costume room will aways be easy to use and easy to take care of.

In each play you give, you need costumes which are right for it; but you will discover that you can re-use your costumes by making them over to fit many different plays. Material can be dyed or painted. It can be stenciled with designs. Sewing can be done with big needles and coarse thread. Many costumes do not need to be hemmed. Their edges can be cut into scallops or fringe, or notched with pinking scissors. Many parts of costumes can be securely pinned, stapled, wired or glued.

Study each play to know the right costumes for it. Costumes should tell the audience what country the play is in, what time in history, and sometimes the time of year and even the time of day. They often tell what age an actor is and what his profession is, and whether he is funny or dignified. Study pictures in costume books and in museums and art galleries to find out how people dressed at the time and place of your story. Start a scrapbook in which you can paste magazine pictures which give you good ideas for costumes and make-up, and in which you can keep your own sketches and designs.

Everyone in your group should help get costumes for each play and items to add to your permanent collection. All kinds of things will be useful to you which are not useful to anyone else—clothing which is out of style or outgrown or outworn is exactly the sort of thing which makes the best costumes.

You could never afford to buy costumes fit for a king. But you can have costumes fit for a king and all his court by collecting from attics old party dresses, bathrobes, capes, skirts, jackets, blouses, curtains, bedspreads and drapes and fashioning them into the right period for your play by adding appropriate sleeves, flounces, trains, sashes, ruffles; trimmings of silk, satin, lace, brocade, velvet, braid; and decorations of beads, buttons, buckles, jewels, feathers and furs. With bits of fancy trimmings, foil, glitter and paint, you will turn socks, oilcloth and old bedroom slippers into rolled-top boots, leggings and fancy slippers. You will make old felt hats, or pieces of cardboard, into regal headpieces: high-peaked cones with veils, pointed caps with feathers, wide-brimmed hats with plumes, brimless hats with tassels, jeweled circlets, gold and silver bands, high scalloped or jagged-edged crowns.

Your village and peasant women will need skirts and blouses of all kinds and colors to wear with shawls and scarves and aprons. Their men will need old pants which can be cut off and buckled below the knee, or tucked into high socks; and smocks and old shirts cut off square at the bottom and belted in at the waist.

Bath towels make tunics for shepherd boys, or turbans for Orientals, or stuffing for clowns, giants and animals.

Tights, long underwear, knit pajama pants and long stockings are good for knights, medieval princes, Robin Hood's men, elves, goblins, animals and insects. Top them with leotards, or knitted pullover shirts, or tight sweaters. For knights, add cardboard armor; for Robin Hood's men, add sleeveless tunics; for princes, add shoulder capes and fancy belts; for goblins and elves, add little gauze or cardboard wings and peaked caps; for animals and insects, add tails or wings, socks for paws, and hoods with the right kinds of ears or antennae.

Costumes for dragons, horses or snowmen can be built on chicken-wire frames covered with cloth. Chicken wire also makes an excellent base for big stiff skirts.

Make-up

Strong stage lighting takes the color out of actors' faces. One reason for using make-up is to put their color back. This use of make-up accents an actor's own natural coloring. You should put on your make-up in the kind of light you will have in your play.

The other use of make-up is to make you different from yourself and like the character you are acting in your play. An elf might have pointed eyebrows; Huckleberry Finn might have freckles and a smudgy face; a doll might have round red cheeks; a soldier might have a tiny painted mustache; a professor might have a little pointed beard. These things can be done with lipsticks, eyebrow pencils and a few grease-paint colors which can be bought in little tins at a drugstore, ten-cent store, or theatrical-supply house.

Color, in make-up, is used for accenting and shadowing. Put the light colors where you want things to be accented, and shadow them carefully with a darker color. To make a nose look long, put a white line down the length of it, and blend a bit of darker color along the sides of the nose. To make a nose look short, color the end of it with a light color, and shadow the bridge a bit, so that the nose is foreshortened. To age your face, highlight your cheekbones, and carefully shade the cheeks themselves with gray eyeshadow. Blend some of the same shadow under your eyes and on your temples. Take the color out of your eyebrows and lips with a little of the same gray. With a gray eyebrow pencil lightly trace your natural "grin lines" and "frown lines." Do not use black for lines or shadows; it is harsh and artificial looking. Whiten your hair above your temples with cornstarch or powder or liquid white shoe polish, and put streaks of white in your hair. And don't forget that if you age your face, you must also age your hands and your neck.

Make-up is fun to do, but it must be done very carefully. A parent or teacher who has had make-up experience can help you learn the art of it. And whatever tricks you use, be very sure to try them out in rehearsals, so you will know that they are right.

You can keep your make-up supplies in a box in your costume room. After you are in costume for your play, put on your make-up in a place where there is good strong light, and where there are mirrors and wastebaskets, and where, if possible, water is available.

The simple supplies which you will need are:

LIPSTICKS. Each actor should have his own, with his name on it.

CAKE ROUGE. Apply it with a puff of cotton.

GREASEPAINT LINERS. The most useful ones are black, gray, brown, blue, green, white.

HAIRPINS.

SCISSORS.

COMB and BRUSH for each actor.

CORNSTARCH, WHITE TALCUM POWDER or LIQUID WHITE SHOE POLISH to whiten hair.

MINERAL OIL, ALBOLENE or COLD CREAM to take make-up off.

FACIAL TISSUES. Many of them.

SOAP.

Have a box for Halloween noses, ears, mustaches, fingernails and other things which you may collect.

You will also want to have material to make beards and wigs. String mops, yarn, cotton and rope can be made into good wigs, beards and manes. Long stockings make good hair and braids. The most realistic mustaches and beards are made from "crepe hair." You can buy this in different colors in lengths of tight braids. Cut off a bit, unravel it, paste it on with spirit gum, and trim it to the shape you want. Take it off carefully with alcohol. It is difficult and usually unsatisfactory to try to make a full wig. It is always better, if possible, to attach hair to a cap or hat or bonnet or other head covering.

PUBLICITY SUPPLIES

You will probably not have an office of your own. But you can have a bulletin board, neatly edged with surplus thumbtacks, for notices to your own group; and a desk in which to keep supplies for making tickets, programs and posters, and in which to keep lists, files, notebooks and scrapbooks. You will need glue, scissors, cellophane tape, rulers, pencils, paints, pens and brushes, as well as your paper supplies. Try to acquire a stapler and an alphabet stencil or stamp set. These are most useful and inexpensive investments.

HOUSEKEEPING SUPPLIES

You should have a closet or corner for housekeeping supplies such as brooms, mops, buckets, cans, cleansers, polish, cloths and sponges. Keep your quarters neat and tidy all of the time. Have a big cleanup after each play, when everything is put away in good condition and your rooms are thoroughly cleaned. Make this job fun instead of work by having a cleanup party as a celebration after each play.

THE PLAYS

Here are some plays which have been selected from dozens that were created by a group of children who met after school one afternoon a week. Each play is followed by production notes which will explain how the scenery, costumes, props, lights and special effects were worked out. The plays were presented to audiences of friends and relatives, without admission charge.

The same plays could be adapted to any number of actors, and could be played in an attic, garage, barn, classroom, auditorium, porch, back yard, garden, playground, or at camp.

In order to make any one of these plays useful for your own particular group, you should start with the story itself and answer the "how do we do it" questions in your own way. These scripts will show you the way one group answered its questions and will suggest other answers, which may be the right ones for you.

ARTHUR'S SWORD

ARTHUR'S SWORD

A dramatization based on the Arthurian Legends

CHARACTERS

MINSTREL	SIR EUSTACE
LADY HELEN	SIR WILLIAM
LADY KATHERINE	SIR RONALD
LADY ELAINE	SIR THOMAS
LADY ROWENA	SIR KAY
LADY MARTHA	SIR HECTOR
LADY MARIAN	MERLIN
SIR RICHARD	ARTHUR

The scene is near the tournament field in the days of Knights and Ladies in Old England. There are moss-covered slopes at each side of the open stage. Centered, at the back of the stage, is a giant stone in which is embedded a beautiful sword. There is no one on the stage as the play starts; but there is the sound of armor clashing, people cheering and trumpets blaring from off-stage left where the KNIGHTS *are finishing their tournament. As these sounds die down, a* MINSTREL *wanders down the aisle toward stage right. He is strumming his lute and singing a song about his journeyings. As he approaches the steps of the stage, he stops singing because he has seen the sword in the stone. He goes to it in amazement and reads the words which are written on the handle of the sword.*

MINSTREL. "Who so pulleth out this sword of this stone is rightwise King born of England." (*He tugs at it.*) Well, I am still a wandering minstrel and *not* the King of England! (*He hears the voices of the* LADIES, *and moves to downstage left to watch them.*)

(*The* LADIES *talk as they enter. They form excited and gossipy groups on the mossy banks at either side of the stage.*)

LADY HELEN. What an exciting tournament it was! And my Sir Richard so gallant! He wore my colors with such bravery!

LADY KATHERINE. Sir Richard indeed! Did you not see Sir Eustace? I think it may be he who moves the sword.

LADY ELAINE (*laughing*). Sir Eustace? If he were King of England, a merry time we'd have! (*The others laugh.*)

LADY ROWENA (*bowing deeply*). And you, dear Lady Katherine, might then be Queen? (*She shakes her finger.*) Fie on it!

LADY MARTHA. Well, we may soon see. For 'tis time they gathered for the tests.

LADY MARIAN. If my Sir Kay had not broken his sword in his fierce jousting, he would have won the whole tournament!

MINSTREL. That was bad fortune indeed. Could he not have replaced his sword?

LADY MARIAN. Aye. He sent his squire, who is his younger brother, to fetch another sword, but he did not return in time.

LADY HELEN. Could it really be today that someone will lift the sword from the stone?

LADY KATHERINE. Oh, I think it will be never! Every Lord in England has already tried.

LADY ELAINE (*runs to the stone and pulls at the sword*). It still is very solid, after all the trials!

LADY ROWENA (*horrified*). You should not touch it, Lady Elaine!

LADY MARTHA (*wags her finger mockingly*). Merlin might magic you into a rabbit, if he saw!

MINSTREL. Pray pardon me, my Ladies. But is there to be a trial here today?

LADY HELEN. You must come from afar, not to know.

MINSTREL. Aye, from afar. I know but little of this land, England.

LADY KATHERINE. You must know how our dear land is torn with strife because we have no King.

MINSTREL. I know the great King Uther has been dead for many a year.

LADY ELAINE. Aye, 18 years the Knights and Barons have been fighting for his throne.

LADY ROWENA. We cannot remember harmony and peace.

MINSTREL. And this sword? Methinks, now, there is a tale about a sword!

LADY MARTHA (*going to the sword and reading*). "Who so pulleth out this sword of this stone is rightwise King born of England."

MINSTREL. King *born* of England? Was there, then, a son?

LADY MARIAN. *Perhaps* there was a son!

MINSTREL. Then why does he not assert his rights?

LADY HELEN. It is a tale of strangeness. . . .

LADY KATHERINE (*interrupting*). 'Tis said there was a son. . . .

LADY ELAINE (*eager to add her bit*). And dear King Uther, dying, feared for the little child. . . .

LADY ROWENA (*eagerly*). Lest he, being weak and small, would be killed by some ambitious Lord or Baron. . . .

LADY MARTHA (*getting her part of the tale in*). And so the great enchanter, Merlin, spirited him away to keep him safe. . . .

LADY MARIAN. Until he would be old enough to rule with power. . . .

MINSTREL. 'Tis indeed a tale of strangeness.

LADY HELEN. And then the sword appeared with this inscription. . . .

LADY KATHERINE. And every day of tournament, the trials are held to find the rightful King. (*Trumpets and the sound of marching interrupt the story.*)

LADY ELAINE (*looking off left*). They are coming now from the pavilions!

LADY ROWENA. Enough then of this chatter. Let us greet them!

(*The* LADIES, *adjusting their trains and their hats in the manner of all ladies waiting for their gentlemen, form a semicircle which has the stone as its center. They watch the* KNIGHTS *coming.*)

LADY MARTHA. How handsome my Lord Thomas is!

LADY MARIAN (*sadly*). Sir Kay is holding still his broken sword!

(*The* KNIGHTS *now march in from stage left. Each one goes to his own fair Lady and kneels before her. The* LADIES *bow.*)

SIR RICHARD. Fair Lady Helen, your colors gave me courage!

SIR EUSTACE. Dear Lady Katherine, the sun shining on my shield was dimmed by the brightness of your eyes!

SIR WILLIAM. Dear Lady Elaine, as I charged my foe, the wind was your voice in my ear.

SIR RONALD. My Lady Rowena, I trust you saw how easily I tilted to my opponent's sorrow! It was with your name on my lips!

SIR THOMAS. My fair Lady Martha, your name was on my lips and in my heart!

SIR KAY. Dear Lady Marian, I return to you with a broken sword!

(*The* KNIGHTS *now rise, seat their* LADIES *on the mossy banks, and then stand behind them.*)

SIR HECTOR (*who has entered last, now walks to the side of the stone and turns to* SIR KAY). Dear Kay, my son, you had bitter luck. But your sword was broken in a great trial of strength and valor. It seemed that the tourney would be yours, but that your sword snapped and left you weaponless.

SIR KAY. I sent my brother to find another sword, but he has not returned in time.

MERLIN (*striding down the center aisle of the audience, as he calls out*). How now, my Lords! Great Lords, good Lords and gracious Ladies! (*He mounts the stage and walks through the circle of bowing* LORDS *and* LADIES, *and takes his position on a step at the left of the great stone.*) The time grows short. This England, split and ravished and made waste by all the fighting and the jealousies, must have a King. A rightful King! Take places, then. The trial of the sword is once more to begin. I am old and have seen much, and much more can foresee. But I fear for this land, this England. O beware, if the rightful King does not come soon and take his place as ruler of this land. So attend! "Who so pulleth out this sword of this stone is rightwise King born of England." Are you ready, my Lords?

LORDS. Aye.

MERLIN. Sir Hector?

SIR HECTOR. Nay, my good Merlin. Do not mock my years. You know I will not try.

MERLIN. Then your son, Sir Kay.

SIR KAY. Well do I need a sword! (*He throws down his broken sword and kneels to* LADY MARIAN, *who has risen. He then mounts the step and pulls at the sword hilt. The others watch breathlessly, and there is a great sigh as he turns aside.*) 'Tis

· 39 ·

not here that I will find a substitute. (*He returns to his place and picks up his broken sword ruefully.* LADY MARIAN *sits sadly.*)

MERLIN. Sir Eustace!

SIR EUSTACE (*kneels before* LADY KATHERINE, *who has risen*). With your prayer, Lady Katherine.

(*The same action of each* KNIGHT, *in turn, kneeling to his own fair* LADY, *mounting the step at the base of the stone, failing to pull the sword from the stone and returning to his place is repeated until all have tried.*)

MERLIN. Sir Richard!

SIR RICHARD. Fair Lady Helen, again give me courage!

MERLIN. Sir William!

SIR WILLIAM. My Lady Elaine, would you might be Queen!

MERLIN. Sir Ronald!

SIR RONALD. Lady Rowena, for you and England!

MERLIN. Sir Thomas!

SIR THOMAS. My Lady Martha, hold me in your thoughts!

MERLIN (*after they have all tried and failed*). This land must be delivered from its strife unto its lawful heir! Post now another Tournament and Trial for three moons hence. And send far and wide for all the Knights to come. But now, attend! Before we leave this hallowed and mystic spot, kneel all, and pray that the rightful King will come not too late! (*All kneel, except* MERLIN.)

ARTHUR (*runs down the center aisle of the audience. As he calls out, the* LORDS *and* LADIES *rise in dismay at this interruption*). Am I too late? Dear Father, and dear Brother, I have not found another sword, and now I see the tourney's over and I am too late!

MERLIN. Who is this lad who runs thus hot and hasty into a sacred place?

SIR HECTOR. By your gracious leave, he is my second son, and Sir Kay's squire. Please pardon him his youth. He means well, and had gone to try to find another sword for Kay, who had broken his on the field. I pray you, forgive his breaking in so rashly!

SIR KAY. A fine time he's been too—and now comes empty-handed and empty-headed!

ARTHUR (*kneeling in front of* MERLIN). This is the great Merlin! Your pardon, sire!

MERLIN (*walks to the kneeling boy*). You are a comely lad. Rise up! You seek a sword for your brother? (*He walks back to his place by the great stone and turns to* ARTHUR.) Hmmmmm! There is an unused sword here.

ALL. No! No!

SIR KAY. Your pardon, great Merlin, you cannot mean to let the hilt of that great sword be touched by this child!

SIR WILLIAM. He has not earned the right to try!

SIR EUSTACE. What mean you, Merlin, to insult us with this child's play?

SIR RICHARD. I will not wait to see such blasphemy. Come, Lady Helen!

SIR RONALD. My hand, Lady Rowena!

SIR THOMAS. This is a jest! He cannot mean to let him try!

MERLIN (*thunders above the commotion*). Silence! Silence!

(*The* KNIGHTS *who are about to lead their* LADIES *away hesitate.*) You glorious Knights who call yourselves chivalrous, attend! (*to* ARTHUR) You say you seek a sword. Will you take this one, perhaps?

ARTHUR (*walks to the stone slowly and stands looking at the sword*). It is a beautiful sword! Worthy of my valiant brother. You say it is unused and I might have it for him? This is indeed a great and wonderful fortune. But 'tis now too late for him to use it. I fear you do make sport of me. The tourney's over now.

MERLIN. We will replay the tourney, if this sword will help you. (*The others laugh scornfully.*)

ARTHUR. You will give my brother Kay another chance? Oh, great good luck! Kay, I will get it for you and you will have another chance! (*He mounts the step in front of the stone and easily pulls out the sword.*) Here is this lovely sword for you, my brother! (*He turns to bring the sword to* KAY *and sees that everyone, except* MERLIN, *is kneeling. He stands there, sword in hand, puzzled.*)

ALL. It is the will of God!

ARTHUR (*to* MERLIN). What means this, sire? Why do they kneel?

MERLIN (*gently*). They kneel to you, my lad. (*He kneels.*) My King!

ALL. Hail to our King! King Arthur!

ARTHUR (*going to* SIR HECTOR). My Father, do not kneel. But tell me what this means!

SIR HECTOR (*rising with* ARTHUR'S *help*). My son, now you must know. You have been my son in my love and in my heart—and will be always. But not my son in fact! You were brought to me as an orphaned child, and I have nurtured you these many years until even I have forgotten you are not my son by blood.

ARTHUR. But I cannot bear this to be true!

MERLIN (*rises*). You cannot bear this to be true? Know you, then, that you are Uther's son, his rightful heir, and now our King! The days of strife are over. You will quell the strife and bring justice and peace to all the land. And all your people will love you, and the fame of your good deeds will shine long after all those who here kneel to you have been forgotten!

ALL (*rising*). Long Live King Arthur!

MINSTREL (*strums his lute*). And many will sing the story and the glory of such a King. But I will be the FIRST to sing it!

(*He starts a song about the sword in the stone. As he sings and all the others bow to their new King, the* CURTAIN *closes.*)

PRODUCTION NOTES

We needed only our blue-sky curtain at the back of the stage and trees at the side for the scenery in this play. The important thing was the stone with its magic sword. We nailed a big box to a small platform, covered both with canvas, and painted the canvas light gray, streaked to look like marble. In the top of the box we cut a slit for the sword. We made the sword out of a piece of wood whittled to a point, sanded, and painted with aluminum paint. The handle was a crosspiece of wood to which we fastened a curved piece of tin to make a hilt. On this we glued glass jewels. The hilt of the sword was toward the audience, so that each person who pulled at the sword stood on the little platform with his back to the audience and braced himself by putting one foot on top of the stone. He looked as if he were tugging with all his strength, when he was really pushing against the stone, so that he wouldn't accidentally pull the sword out. Arthur, of course, pulled it out very easily.

To make all the action and the meaning of the play focus on this stone, we placed it in the center at the back of the stage. To emphasize its importance, we stood a screen behind it, which we covered with a velvet drape. On the drape we pinned a cardboard shield painted with heraldic designs. To the top of the screen we fastened two long trumpets with banners.

On either side of the stone we put sections of rock wall. We used these rock walls in many of our plays. They were little screens about three feet high and three feet long, painted gray with markings of soft brown, shadowed between the rocks with dark blue, and hinged together so they would stand alone.

We put a section of our steps on each side of the stage and slanted them toward the stone. These we covered with dark-green drapes to look like mossy slopes. This is where the Ladies and Knights grouped themselves to watch the Trial of the Sword. We also used sections of our steps at the front of the stage, so actors could enter from the audience. Merlin stood above the others on a small box painted to look like a rock, beside the giant stone. The Minstrel sat on another box-rock at the front corner of the stage.

The Ladies made their costumes out of evening dresses or long skirts and fancy blouses. The tops of the skirts were safety-pinned high and covered with wide sashes. Some of the Ladies had long scarves or laces hanging from the back of the neck to the floor. They wore ballet slippers or soft sandals on their feet. Each Lady made her own hat out of a big piece of colored blotting paper shaped into a tall cone and stapled. A piece of silk or a scarf fluttered from the tip of the cone.

The Knights wore tights and long-sleeved pullover sweaters or knit shirts. Over his costume each Knight wore a long piece of velvet, sateen or other rich-looking material with a hole cut in it for his head. He belted this in with a fancy belt. He made a coat of arms of his own and pinned it to the front of his costume. He wore soft sandals or bedroom slippers or sock boots on his feet and laced his legs with leather thongs or with ribbon. Around his arm he wore ribbons the color of his Lady's scarf. The Knights did not wear armor, because they would have taken it off at their pavilions when the tournament was over, before the play started.

Arthur wore tights and a long-sleeved knit shirt with a belt.

Sir Hector, who was older than the other Knights, wore a long velvet evening cape, belted in with a long cord. To a bathing cap (for a bald head) he pasted hair made of raveled rope. His beard was raveled rope fastened to a cord which tied over his ears.

Merlin's full floor-length robe was black, roped in at the waist. It had once been an academic gown. On it were sewn cutouts of white owls, stars and crescent moons. His tall, peaked hat, with more white cutouts, was made of black blotting paper. To his hat was attached long white string hair and beard.

The Minstrel wore tights, a belted smock and sock boots, and a felt hat with a feather. He made a sturdy lute, so we could use it in other plays. He attached a round hatbox to a long wooden handle which had a headpiece on it. The headpiece was made out of cardboard with tuning keys on either side of it. He stretched wires from the tuning keys, the length of the handle, and over a hole he had cut in the hatbox. After it was painted, he tied colored streamers to it and attached a wide ribbon for a sling to carry it over his shoulder. He made up the words and tunes of his songs after we had all listened to records of the ballads of the days of chivalry and had sung some from a music book of early folk tunes.

There were sixteen actors. If you have more players, you can add lines for them. Or to have fewer Knights and Ladies, you could take out some of the lines or combine them into longer speeches for each person. If you want a longer and more elaborate play, you might start it with the Knights going to the Tournament, or with a scene at the pavilions where the Knights are taking off their armor at the end of the Tournament. Or you might have a scene in which Sir Kay sends Arthur to get another sword.

It would be an exciting outdoor play with the Knights and Ladies, with banners, flags and trumpets, coming in processions from the distance. At camp you might even have a scene at the Tournament with your best horsemen really jousting; or, if this is too difficult or dangerous, a single herald might ride in bringing the news of the Trial of the Sword to the countryside and leading the audience to the playing site, and then galloping off to lead the Knights in from the Tournament.

If you play it outdoors, plan the speeches so that the Ladies can speak together and the Knights can speak together, and let most of the play be pantomime, except for Merlin, who might cup his hands like a megaphone when he makes his pronouncements. Or you might have a group of minstrels who tell the story of the legend as the actors act it.

Other stories about King Arthur could be added to this one and make a project for a whole summer at camp or playground. The story of chivalry, with its rich costuming, its exciting action and its music would provide many hours of research, work and fun.

SUPPOSE

SUPPOSE

An original play

(With thanks to Charlotte Stoddard,
who helped write the script)

CHARACTERS

NUMBER ONE, who embroiders linen
NUMBER TWO, who writes poetry
NUMBER THREE, who draws pictures
NUMBER FOUR, who plays the lute
NUMBER FIVE, who weaves garlands
NUMBER SIX, who paints china
NUMBER SEVEN, who cooks and mends
and cleans
COURTIERS, who are very elegant
COURT LADIES, who are even more so
HERALDS, who are even MORE so,
if possible
THE KING, who is wise

*The scene is on the way to the palace. As the curtain opens to
the music of the* Second Movement *of the Mozart* Sonata No.
34 *in F Major, Part II, seven girls are sitting in a row on stools
at the back of the stage. Six of them are dressed alike and very
beautifully. But* NUMBER SEVEN, *at the stage-right end of the
line-up, wears a simple brown dress. At her side is a table with
housekeeping supplies on it.* NUMBER ONE *is embroidering.*
NUMBER TWO *is writing on a parchment scroll with a quill pen.*
NUMBER THREE *is sketching a picture.* NUMBER FOUR *is strumming a lute.* NUMBER FIVE *is braiding a flower garland.* NUM-

BER SIX *is painting a china plate.* NUMBER SEVEN *is stirring batter. The music diminishes, as the girls speak.*

1. Here we sit
2. And sit
3. And sit
4. And sit
5. And sit
6. And sit

1. Sewing stitches ..... Ah! (*big sigh*).
2. Writing poems ...... Ah! (*big sigh*).
3. Drawing pictures .... Ah! (*big sigh*).
4. Playing music ...... Ah! (*big sigh*).
5. Weaving garlands ... Ah! (*big sigh*).
6. Painting china ...... Ah! (*big sigh*).

ALL 6. How dull!

7. There is so much to do, I'm too busy to be dull!

ALL 6 (*pausing in their activities*). Yes?

7 (*stirring the batter*). Cooking . . .

ALL 6 (*disgusted*). Oh!

7 (*mending breeches*). Mending . . .

ALL 6 (*more disgusted*). Oh!

7 (*dusting the table*). Cleaning . . .

ALL 6 (*most disgusted*). Never!!

1. For I must stitch (*does so*).
2. And I must write (*does so*).
3. And I must draw (*does so*).
4. And I must play (*does so*).
5. And I must weave (*does so*).
6. And I must paint (*does so*).

7. But why?

1 (*turning to* 2). Suppose . . .
2 (*turning to* 3). Suppose . . .
3 (*turning to* 4). Suppose . . .
4 (*turning to* 5). Suppose . . .
5 (*turning to* 6). Suppose . . .
6 (*turning to* 7). Suppose . . .

ALL 6 (*facing front*). A King Comes By!

7. What then?

ALL 6. Why then we'd wed! (*Each looks at the others in surprise and says in turn*) What YOU? No, no he'd marry ME!

1. He'd see my patterns.

ALL 5 (*condescendingly*). Patterns!

2. He'd read my lines.

ALL 5 (*condescendingly*). Lines!

3. He'd watch me draw.

ALL 5 (*condescendingly*). Draw!

4. He'd hear my tunes.

ALL 5 (*condescendingly*). Tunes!

5. He'd wear my garlands.

ALL 5 (*condescendingly*). Garlands!

6. He'd like my china.

ALL 5 (*condescendingly*). China!

7 (*wistfully*). Ho hum! He'd never notice me!

ALL 6. Of course not!!

7. But someone has to cook . . .

ALL 6 (*nodding*). Yes.

7. And mend . . .

ALL 6 (*nodding*). Yes.

7. And clean . . .

ALL 6 (*nodding*). Yes.

7. And anyway I like to serve the ones I love!

ALL 6 (*haughtily*). But not I!

1. For I must stitch.
2. And I must write.
3. And I must draw.
4. And I must play.
5. And I must weave.
6. And I must paint.

ALL 6. Because . . .

1 (*turning to 2*). Suppose . . .
2 (*turning to 3*). Suppose . . .
3 (*turning to 4*). Suppose . . .
4 (*turning to 5*). Suppose . . .
5 (*turning to 6*). Suppose . . .
6 (*turning to 7*). Suppose . . .

ALL 6 (*facing front*). A King Comes By!

> (*There is a sudden flourish of trumpets. The music changes to the* Rondo *of the Mozart Sonata, Third Movement. Down the center aisle through the audience march the* COURTIERS. *They are dressed in the fanciest extreme of courtly style. They march to the stage and line up across it, facing the audience. They pay no attention to the seven girls who are now hidden behind these gallants. Following the* COURTIERS *come the* COURT LADIES, *elegant and sophisticated. They line up facing the* COURTIERS. *They have their backs to the audience, but their backs are very expressive. With their left hands they hold their skirts. With*

their right hands they hold their oversized lorgnettes. Stop music.)

COURTIERS (*addressing the* COURT LADIES *and the audience*). Have you heard the latest news?

COURT LADIES. Do tell!

COURTIERS. The King . . .

COURT LADIES. Yes?

COURTIERS. The King . . .

COURT LADIES. Yes??

COURTIERS. The King will not have Lady Sue, though she can dance so neatly!

LADY SUE (*the center* COURT LADY). Though I can dance so neatly! (*She pirouettes in place.*)

COURT LADIES (*pirouetting in place*). Though she can dance so neatly!

COURTIERS. The King will not have Lady Prue, though she can sing so sweetly!

LADY PRUE. Though I can sing so sweetly, (*trills*) tra, la, la, la, la!

COURT LADIES. Though she can sing so sweetly, tra, la, la, la, la!

COURTIERS. The King will not have Fair Elaine, though she is regal with her train!

FAIR ELAINE (*sweeping her train*). Though I am regal with my train!

COURT LADIES (*sweeping their trains*). Though she is regal with her train!

COURTIERS. The King will not have Lady May, though she is champion at croquet!

LADY MAY (*swinging an imaginary mallet*). Though I am champion at croquet!

COURT LADIES (*swinging imaginary mallets*). Though she is champion at croquet!

COURTIERS. He still is searching for a bride . . .

COURT LADIES. He's searched the kingdom far and wide . . .

COURTIERS AND LADIES. And still he is not satisfied!

> (*Again the trumpets sound off stage. But now the trumpets enter, and they are long and beautiful trumpets carried proudly by strutting* HERALDS. *The* HERALDS *move down the center aisle through the audience as the* COURTIERS *and* COURT LADIES—*by stepping to the right and left—give room for the* HERALDS *at center front of stage.*)

HERALDS. The King comes here! Make Way! Make Way! Prepare yourselves without delay! He seeks a queen this very day!

COURTIERS AND LADIES. The King comes here?

HERALDS. The King comes here!

COURTIERS AND LADIES. To find a Queen?

HERALDS. To find a Queen!

COURT LADIES (*turning to each other in great excitement*). Suppose, suppose, suppose, suppose, suppose, suppose . . .

HERALDS. But he is very hard to please!

COURTIERS. We've begged and begged him on our knees!

COURT LADIES. If we *knew* what to do, we'd do our best to pass the test!

HERALDS. But he is very hard to please!

COURTIERS. We've begged and begged him on our knees!

(The HERALDS *now raise their trumpets and blow a mighty flourish, for indeed comes the* KING. *He walks down the center aisle. He carries a parchment scroll which he is sadly contemplating. The* COURT LADIES *bow to the floor. The* COURTIERS *and* HERALDS *stand at attention. The* KING *mounts the stage and stands center between the* HERALDS *who have respectfully given him room.)*

KING. *(He reads from his scroll. After each name, he draws a line through that one with his quill.)*

> The Countess Carramba of Carapay,
> The Princess Paramba of Paraguay,
> The Lady Matilda, the Duchess of Dilda,
> The Dowager Queen of Dupray,
> Cora and Dora and Flora and Laura,
> Lottie and Dottie and Nan,
> Betty and Vetty and Letty and Netty,
> Polly and Molly and Ann,
> Lady Sue . . .

LADY SUE *(bowing)*. I danced for you . . .

COURT. 'Tis true.

KING. Lady Prue . . .

LADY PRUE *(bowing)*. I sang for you . . .

COURT. 'Tis true.

KING. Lady May . . .

LADY MAY *(bowing)*. I played croquet for you . . .

COURT. 'Tis true.

KING. Fair Elaine . . .

FAIR ELAINE. I walked for you . . .

COURT. 'Tis true.

(The KING *hands his scroll to the nearest* HERALD.*)*

HERALDS AND COURTIERS. You've drawn a line through every name. There are no others. What a shame!

(*The* HERALDS *and* COURTIERS *and* COURT LADIES, *all in sorrow, sadly move away in withdrawal to the sides of the stage. This movement reveals the* SEVEN GIRLS *who have been sitting quietly all the time. Softly the music of the Mozart* Second Movement *is heard. This is the girls' motif.*)

KING. But who are these? (*He walks to stage left and looks at the line of the seven of them.*)

1. I'm Violetta Marigold.
2. I'm Violetta Gay.
3. I'm Violet Evangelina Morninglory May.
4. I'm Violetta Eleanor.
5. I'm Violet Lorraine.
6. I'm Violet Belinda Bell.

7 (*after a slight pause*). And I'm Plain Jane.

KING. These names are new! What do you do?

1. I embroider the finest linen!

COURT (*with interest*). Finest linen!

2. My poetry is of the utmost elegance!

COURT. Utmost elegance!

3. There are no words to describe the quality of my drawing!

COURT. Drawing!

4. No one has ever plucked a lute with such discrimination.

COURT. Discrimination!

5. Have you ever seen garlands more exquisite?

COURT. More exquisite!

6. Or finer brushwork on delicate china?

COURT. Delicate china!

KING (*looking at* SEVEN, *who modestly hangs her head*). And you?

ALL 6. She has no talent!

7. No talent.

COURT (*horrified*). No talent!!

KING (*eagerly*). No talent??

ALL 6. She cooks and mends and cleans!

7. I cook and mend and clean.

COURT (*more horrified*). She cooks and mends and cleans!!!!

KING (*more eagerly*). You cook and mend and clean?????

ALL 6. Yes! She takes care of us.

1. So that I may stitch . . .
2. And I may write . . .
3. And I may draw . . .
4. And I may play . . .
5. And I may weave . . .
6. And I may paint . . .

KING (*with greatest interest*). And why is this?

COURT. Yes, why is this?

7. But someone has to cook . . .

COURT. Yes.

7. And mend . . .

COURT. Yes.

7. And clean . . .

COURT. Yes.

7. And anyway I like to serve the ones I love.

KING (*crosses to her and kneels*). At last one lady on the scene who is worthy to be Queen! Lady, your hand. If you agree, I'd like to have you marry me!

(*She takes his hand and rises to stand beside him.*)

COURT (*in such amazement*). Who would have guessed *that* was the test????

COURT LADIES (*to each other*). If we had only known, we might be on the throne!

ALL 6 (*looking straight ahead*). What's the use of what we've practiced?

1. It's not enough to stitch . . .
2. Or write . . .
3. Or draw . . .
4. Or play . . .
5. Or weave . . .
6. Or paint . . .

1 AND 2 (*together*). Sister dear . . .

7. Yes?

1 AND 2. If you will teach us how to cook . . .

1. I'll embroider your bridal veil!

2. I'll tell your royal romance in rhyme!

3 AND 4 (*together*). Sister dear . . .

7. Yes?

3 AND 4. If you will teach us how to mend . . .

3. I'll draw a picture of the coronation!

4. I'll play the music for your wedding march!

5 AND 6 (*together*). Sister dear . . .

7. Yes?

5 AND 6. If you will teach us how to clean . . .

5. I'll weave the garlands which will deck the hall!

6. I'll paint the china for the marriage feast!

7 (*to all of them, so gracefully*). Of course I will!

ALL 6. Oh, thank you, Sister dear!

KING (*raising his hand—the one which isn't holding* JANE'S).
One moment, my dears! Here's the moral of this story. . . .
Do not do these things for glory!

ALL 6 (*so humbly*). Yes, your Majesty!

> (*The music of the* Don Giovanni Minuet *swells through
> the theater. The* KING *and* JANE *step neatly to the music
> down the center aisle of the audience. The* HERALDS *and
> the* COURTIERS *follow, each with a* COURT LADY *for a part-
> ner. In a double line the Court thus moves off to the castle
> and the wedding festivities. But on the stage there are still
> the* SIX GIRLS *on their six stools. They have watched the
> recessional sadly. Now the music changes to the Mozart
> Second Movement. The girls look at each other. Then
> they all rise and put their artistic props under their stools.
> They walk in single file to the little table at stage right.
> Each one picks up a prop from the table and comes back
> to her stool. They sit.*)

1. Here we sit
2. And sit
3. And sit
4. And sit
5. And sit
6. And sit

1. Peeling onions . . . . . Ah! (*big sigh*).
2. Stirring batter . . . . . . Ah! (*big sigh*).
3. Darning stockings . . Ah! (*big sigh*).
4. Mending breeches . . Ah! (*big sigh*).

5. Dusting stools . . . . . . Ah! (*big sigh*).
6. Cleaning silver . . . . . Ah! (*big sigh*).

ALL 6. How dull! (*an enormous sigh*) And why? Because . . .

1 (*turning to 2*). Suppose . . .
2 (*turning to 3*). Suppose . . .
3 (*turning to 4*). Suppose . . .
4 (*turning to 5*). Suppose . . .
5 (*turning to 6*). Suppose . . .
6 (*turning to where 7 used to be*). Suppose . . .

ALL 6 (*facing front*). A King Comes By!

(*They are busy at their homely tasks as the* CURTAIN *slowly hides them.*)

PRODUCTION NOTES

This original playlet is very short and needs few rehearsals. The lines are easy, because only Number One has many to remember. The other Sisters simply follow what she says. The play is fun to do because of the rhythm of the speeches and the precise exaggeration of the gestures, actions and posings.

The music helps set the timing for the speech and the action, and also establishes the mood of the play. We used Mozart music, which made the actors feel elegant, graceful, sophisticated and charming. It was perfect music to step to, dance to, and pose to. The *Second Movement* of the Mozart *Sonata No. 34 in F Major, Part II* was the "theme song" of the artistic sisters, and was played very softly whenever they were speaking. The *Rondo* of the same sonata, *Third Movement*, set the mood for the processional entrance of the grand court. To the music of the *Don Giovanni Minuet*, the Ladies and Lords bowed, posed and stepped daintly off in a double line to the wedding.

The costumes had the general feel of the Colonial period of the Mozart music. The Six Artist Sisters were dressed alike in white crinoline petticoats and white blouses, with purple sashes, hairbows and neckerchiefs. Plain Jane wore a brown skirt and blouse. The Court Ladies wore differently colored full skirts and blouses, with decorative trains, jewels and laces. The Courtiers and Heralds were in fancy blouses, ruffs, knee breeches, long stockings and shoes with fancy buckles. Pedal pushers made good knee breeches, tied in below the knee with ribbons. The King added to this costume a crown and a long shoulder cape made of a velvet curtain bordered with a strip of white flannel with painted black markings on it for ermine.

For scenery, we set our sectional rock walls twined with flowers against our sky-curtain. Birds and butterflies hovered overhead.

The only stage props are seven stools and a small table. We used high stools, so that the Sisters' toes, demurely pointed under their crinolines, just touched the floor. You could use boxes or benches instead of stools.

Most of the hand props are easily available ones: a square of white cloth with a big needle and colored embroidery thread; a strip of brown paper for a scroll and a long feather for a quill pen; a drawing pad and pencil; braided artificial flowers; a white plate and a paint brush; a pan of onions; a wooden bowl and spoon; socks; knee breeches; feather duster; silver spoon and polishing cloth.

To learn how we made our lute, read the production notes for *Arthur's Sword*, page 45. If you prefer to use a small harp called a lyre, cut it out of cardboard, string it with wires, and cover the frame with gold foil. This will also be useful in a Biblical or Greek play.

To make a short trumpet, tape a cardboard or tin funnel to a dowel or window-shade roller. For a long one, fasten the funnel to a broom handle. We made our trumpets from bathroom toilet plungers, and they have lasted in perfect condition for 15 years! We painted them gold and hung from them banners made of fringed cloth, painted with heraldic designs. Sometimes, instead of using banners, we tied ribbon streamers to the trumpets.

To make a scroll, staple or glue each end of a long piece of brown wrapping paper or cloth to a chair rung or dowel. Attach a ribbon to one end, so that the scroll can be rolled and tied.

This play was first performed by 35 children, who rehearsed it in six one-hour periods. Since then, it has been played many times by different numbers of actors. Once, at camp, ten girls gave it after three rehearsals. They changed the lines to fit their cast of Seven Sisters, One Herald, One Courtier and the King. The Herald led the camp audience to their surprise play under a big tree one summer evening. One group of teenagers stylized the play by costuming it entirely in black and white. They used no actual props, but suggested them by exaggerated pantomime.

THE POTTED PRINCESS

THE POTTED PRINCESS

A dramatization based on the story by
Rudyard Kipling found in *The St. Nicholas Anthology,*
Random House, New York

CHARACTERS

THE PRINCESS	THE THREE PRINCES
TWO SERVANTS	THE SON OF A POTTER
THE KING	HIS MOTHER
THE QUEEN	A GNOME
THE THREE WISEMEN	THE FAIRY QUEEN

OLD MOTHER WITCH

*The scene is the Courtyard of an Eastern Palace many years
ago. At center stage is a large covered grain jar. At curtain rise,
the music of the* Arab Dance *from the* Nutcracker Suite *is
heard. This continues softly throughout the court scene. The
PRINCESS is dancing, while her TWO SERVANTS, standing right
and left upstage, are beating the time of the music. When the
KING and QUEEN enter, the SERVANTS and the PRINCESS bow to
the floor.*

SCENE ONE

KING. Most beloved Princess, my Royal Daughter, rise!

PRINCESS (*rising*). O most Royal Mother and Father.

QUEEN. My Daughter, we have news for you.

KING. It is time, my Daughter, now you are sixteen, that we
choose a Prince for you.

QUEEN. The most noble men in all the kingdom seek you for
a bride.

KING. But we must be sure that we choose the most worthy.

QUEEN. How can we know which is the best?

KING. I will call my Wisemen. (*He claps his hands. The* SERVANTS *rise up.*) Call my Wisemen.

> (*The* SERVANTS *bow low and go off. They return followed by the* WISEMEN. *These three wizards wear fantastic robes and high headdresses. The first carries a crystal ball. All have long white beards. They walk in single file to the music, with high knee-bend steps and hunched backs. They form a line at stage left facing the* KING *and bow deeply.*)

WISEMEN (*who always speak in a singsong chant*). We come, O King, to do your will.

KING. Tell me who is the most wise and worthy Prince in all my kingdom, that he may marry my Daughter, the Princess.

WISEMEN. Let us examine our magic, your Majesty. (*They walk in a circle, muttering magic. They gaze into the crystal ball.*)

QUEEN. What do you see in the stars in your crystal ball, O Wisemen?

KING. Speak!

WISEMEN. It is written in the stars, O King!

FIRST WISEMAN. The Princess must be shut up in this grain jar of dried clay for a year.

SECOND. Whoever can take her out is the wisest man in all the kingdom.

THIRD. He is worthy to marry her.

PRINCESS (*runs to the* QUEEN). O, most Royal Mother!

QUEEN. But she will die!

WISEMEN. She will not die, O Royal Queen. Our magic is the most powerful.

KING. This is the will of the stars?

WISEMEN. It is the will of the stars, O King.

QUEEN (*embracing the* PRINCESS). Be brave, my Royal Daughter!

KING (*embracing the* PRINCESS). It is written in the stars, my Daughter!

WISEMEN. In the stars, O Princess!

(*The* KING *claps his hands.* SERVANTS *escort the* PRINCESS *to the grain jar and help her into it. Then they put the cover on the jar. The* WISEMEN *circle around the jar weaving spells. Then they stand upstage center behind the grain jar. The* SERVANTS *stand on either side of them.*)

KING. Call the men who wait and wish to marry the Princess.

(SERVANTS *bow and go out. They return at once leading the* THREE PRINCES, *who are followed by the* SON OF THE POTTER. *They go to stage left where they face the* KING *and bow. The* THREE PRINCES *are dressed in the most elaborate oriental finery. The* SON OF THE POTTER *wears a simple short belted robe.*)

KING. You who wish to marry the Princess, listen to the Wisemen.

WISEMEN. It is written in the stars!

FIRST. The Princess must be shut up in this grain jar of dried clay for a year.

SECOND. Whoever can take her out is the wisest man in all the kingdom.

THIRD. He is worthy to marry her.

KING. You have heard! A year from today come back. The one

who can take her out of the jar shall marry her and shall govern ten provinces, and sit upon an elephant with tusks of gold.

THREE PRINCES (*bowing*). We hear, O most Royal King!

KING (*claps hands*). Go through my kingdom and proclaim this news!

> (SERVANTS *bow and go out.* WISEMEN *muttering magic lead the* THREE PRINCES *three times round the jar and then lead them off. The* KING *and* QUEEN—*with sad looks at the jar—follow the procession off. The* SON OF THE POTTER *has stayed behind. The music changes to the* Prince *and* Princess *from* Scheherazade. *The* SON OF THE POTTER *looks longingly at the grain jar. His* MOTHER *enters and comes to him.*)

MOTHER. My Son, why do you stay here looking so sad?

SON OF POTTER. Mother, I wish to marry the Princess.

MOTHER. But why do you stay here?

SON OF POTTER. The King's Wisemen have put the Princess in this grain jar. Whoever can open it at the end of a year can marry her.

MOTHER. And why does that make you sad?

SON OF POTTER. I am only the Son of a poor Potter. I have no money or horses to go to the ends of the earth to find the right magic to open the jar.

MOTHER. Have the other men done this?

SON OF POTTER. They have all gone to find the most powerful magic.

MOTHER. My Son, you are a prince even though you are poor. Remember that a pot is a pot, and thou art the Son of a Potter.

CURTAIN

SCENE TWO

(*Immediately the music of the* Parade of the Grasshoppers *by Prokofiev begins. A* GNOME *dances in from below the stage. He carries an enormous toadstool. He hops up on the steps which are in front of the curtain, center, puts his toadstool down, and curls up beneath it. Over the Gnome music comes the sound of galloping hoofs. Down the center aisle of the audience comes* PRINCE ONE. *He mounts the steps and prods the sleeping* GNOME *with his lance.*)

GNOME (*in a high squeaky voice*). Who disturbs my sleep?

PRINCE ONE. O Magic Gnome, help me, I pray!

GNOME (*petulantly*). Why should I?

PRINCE ONE. Because I wish to marry the Princess.

GNOME. Go marry her and let me sleep.

PRINCE ONE. But I must have the greatest magic in all the world.

GNOME. Then you have come to the right Gnome.

PRINCE ONE. The Princess is shut up in a jar and the one who opens it can marry her.

GNOME. Why should I help you?

PRINCE ONE. Because I am rich and powerful.

GNOME. You are rich?

PRINCE ONE. I will give you anything you ask.

GNOME. Then give me those green beads around your neck.

PRINCE ONE. I cannot give you my beads. They were given me by my great grandmother.

GNOME. Give me your beads!!

PRINCE ONE. Anything else, O Gnome.

GNOME. Give me your beads!!

PRINCE ONE (*reluctantly putting them on the* GNOME'S *neck*). They are yours.

GNOME (*gleefully*). Oh my pretty beads! Lead the way, Prince.

(*The* GNOME, *carrying the toadstool, follows* PRINCE ONE *down center aisle. The Gnome music and hoofbeats fade, and above them is the music of* Evening *by Prokofiev. The* FAIRY QUEEN *dances in and takes her place at the top of the steps. Butterflies and flowers flutter from her filmy wings. As she sways and poses,* PRINCE TWO *gallops down center aisle to her.*)

PRINCE TWO. Queen of the Fairies, at last I have found you! I have gone round the world to find you!

FAIRY QUEEN. And why?

PRINCE TWO. I beg you to help me win the Princess.

FAIRY QUEEN. The one who is in the grain jar?

PRINCE TWO. Yes, O Fairy Queen.

FAIRY QUEEN. And why should I help you?

PRINCE TWO. I will give you anything your heart desires.

FAIRY QUEEN. I have everything I want.

PRINCE TWO. Gold?

FAIRY QUEEN. I have sunbeams of gold.

PRINCE TWO. Silver?

FAIRY QUEEN. I have moonbeams of silver.

PRINCE TWO. Jewels?

FAIRY QUEEN. But see my jewels!

PRINCE TWO. What then?

FAIRY QUEEN. What is that shiny thing you carry?

PRINCE TWO. That is my shield.

FAIRY QUEEN. Give it to me!

PRINCE TWO. But I need my shield.

FAIRY QUEEN. Give it to me. I can look into it and see how beautiful I am.

PRINCE TWO (*reluctantly giving her his shield*). It is yours.

(*The* FAIRY QUEEN *looks into shield as in a mirror and poses. Then she dances off behind* PRINCE TWO *down center aisle. The music changes to the last part of the Tchaikovsky Number Four. The lights flash, thunder rolls, and* OLD MOTHER WITCH *dances on. She carries a steaming cauldron. She comes to the top of the steps and stirs her brew.*)

WITCH (*in a fearful voice*). He, he, he! I am at the end of the world and I brew my magic where no one can see! Frogs' legs, snakes' eyes, dragons' teeth. Brew and bubble and make my magic strong! (*sound of horse galloping*) Who comes here?

PRINCE THREE (*now at the steps*). Old Mother Witch! I have come to the World's End to find you!

WITCH. Go before I put you in my pot! You would make good stew!

PRINCE THREE. But see, Old Witch, what I have brought you from the bottom of the ocean!

WITCH (*squinting at the shiny string he dangles*). Shiny scales of glittering fish! Give them to me!

PRINCE THREE (*holding them away from her clutch*). I will give them to you, Old Witch, if you will help me.

WITCH. Give them to me!!

PRINCE THREE. I will give them to you if you will come with me and work your magic charms on the Potted Princess.

WITCH. Give them to me!

PRINCE THREE. You will come?

WITCH. Give them to me and I will ride through inky night and be there before you.

(*She seizes the fish scales and puts them into her pot. Muttering her magic spells she goes out, as* PRINCE THREE *gallops away.*)

CURTAIN

SCENE THREE

(*The curtains now open. The Courtyard is the same as at the beginning of the play. The music is again the* Arab Dance. *The* TWO SERVANTS *are in their original positions.*)

FIRST SERVANT. A year has gone by since the Princess was put in the pot.

SECOND SERVANT. This is the great day of the tests!

(*The* KING *and* QUEEN *enter followed by the* WISEMEN. KING *and* QUEEN *stand at stage right center. The* WISEMEN *take their positions back of the grain jar, upstage center.*)

KING. This is the day!

WISEMEN. This is the day!

QUEEN. We will see our Daughter again!

KING. Is everything ready for the tests?

WISEMEN. All is ready, O King.

KING (*claps hands*). Bring in those who would marry the Princess.

(SERVANTS *bow and go off. They return leading a proces-sion. Each* PRINCE *is accompanied by his magic helper. After them come the* SON OF THE POTTER *and his* MOTHER. *All form a semicircle stage left and bow.*)

KING. A year has gone by. You have had a chance to find the most powerful magic in the world to open the grain jar. The one who can open the jar will marry the Princess. Choose your turn.

(SERVANTS *bow and then present lots to the* THREE PRINCES. *They ignore the* SON OF THE POTTER.)

MOTHER (*coming center and bowing low*). My Son wishes to have a turn.

KING. But he has brought no magic.

MOTHER. He is a prince, even though he is the Son of a Potter.

SON OF POTTER. I have no magic. I will watch the others. (MOTHER *and* SON *retire down left.*)

KING. Prince Number One, Begin!

(*Stop* Arab Dance *music.*)

PRINCE ONE (*bows*). O King, I have been through fire and flood to find the most powerful magic. I bring a Gnome whose powers are the greatest in the world!

(Grasshopper *music of Prokofiev. The* GNOME *dances around the stage and produces magic tricks from a prop pouch which he carries. He scatters confetti, serpentine, etc., over the jar. Then the* GNOME *bows to the* KING *and stands aside. All gaze at the jar. But nothing happens. Stop music.*)

ALL. It does not open!

WISEMEN. You have failed!

GNOME (*stamping angrily*). What is this magic more powerful than mine? (*sits at edge of stage in disgust*)

KING. Prince Number Two!

PRINCE TWO (*bows*). O King, I have fought the most desperate dragons before I found the Queen of the Fairies. She will weave her spell for me.

> (*Music of* Evening *by Prokofiev.* FAIRY QUEEN *dances, scattering flowers, stars, butterflies, etc. Bird songs are heard through the music.*)

FAIRY QUEEN. Open, pot! I the Queen of the Fairies touch you with my magic wand! (*Stop music. Everyone gazes at the pot. Nothing happens.*)

ALL. It does not open!

WISEMEN. You have failed!

FAIRY QUEEN (*sitting beside the* GNOME). What is this magic more powerful than mine?

KING. Only one Prince is left. Let him try!

PRINCE THREE (*bows*). The Gnome has failed and the Fairy Queen has failed. But I have gone to the uttermost end of the world and have brought the blackest magic from the Oldest Mother of the Oldest Witches. She will not fail!

> (*Witch music. Lightning and thunder and smoke. The* WITCH *dances and mutters her black magic spells. When the music stops, the lights come up and everyone is cowering in terror. But nothing happens.*)

ALL. It does not open!

WISEMEN. You have failed!

> (WITCH, *still muttering, joins the* GNOME *and* FAIRY *in disgrace.*)

KING. You have all failed!

QUEEN. But my Daughter! My Daughter! Is there no one else?

MOTHER (*bows*). There is one more to try. Most Royal Highness, grant my Son leave to try. My Son, the Son of the Potter.

KING. But he has no magic.

MOTHER. I beg you let him try!

QUEEN. Yes, let him try!

THE OTHERS (*in great scorn*). The Son of a Potter!

KING. Let the Son of the Potter come forward.

SON OF POTTER (*coming center and bowing*). I have no magic, my King. But I love your daughter. My Mother has told me a pot is a pot, and I am the Son of a Potter!

(*Music of* Prince and Princess *from* Scheherazade *begins, and continues to the end of the play. The* SON OF THE POTTER *walks to the back of the pot and with both hands he simply lifts the lid. The* PRINCESS *rises. He takes her hand and helps her out of the pot. He leads her to the* KING, *and there the* SON OF THE POTTER *and the* PRINCESS *kneel for the royal blessing.*)

ALL (*in great awe*). This is very great magic indeed!

WISEMEN. This is no magic at all. It *was* a common grain jar; and it *is* a common grain jar.

FIRST WISEMAN. We did not put any charm upon the jar.

SECOND WISEMAN. A child might have lifted the cover one year ago, or on any day since that day.

THIRD WISEMAN. There was no magic. And now one man has taken everything because he was not afraid.

KING. Son of the Potter, you are the wisest man in my kingdom, and you shall marry my Daughter and govern ten provinces, and sit upon an elephant with tusks of gold. You others, go home, or if you will, stay to see the wedding. But remember a pot is just a pot.

ALL (*to audience as the curtains close*). Remember, a pot is just a pot!

CURTAIN

PRODUCTION NOTES

We changed the Kipling story in many ways when we made this play to fit our group. The seven boys in our group wanted to be the King, the Son of the Potter, the Two Servants and the Three Princes. The girls were the Queen, the Princess, the Mother, the Wisemen and the Magic Creatures. The three girls who wanted to be the Magic Creatures decided what kind of magic creatures they wanted to be. This is why we had a Gnome, a Witch and a Fairy Queen.

After you read the Kipling story, you might work out an entirely different cast of characters. You might prefer to have other kinds of magic helpers. You might want to increase the number of characters and lengthen the play by having more Princes and their Magic Creatures, and more Wisemen. If you have fewer actors, you might use only one Servant, one Wiseman and either a King or a Queen instead of both of them.

After we had acted out our play in several ways, we made a script. But the scripts were used very little and were never taken home. All of the actors knew all of the parts, and they all had fun practicing the walk and chant of the Wisemen and helping create the dances for the Magic Creatures.

In this production we hung some colorful drapes and tapestries on the back wall of our stage to make the Courtyard ornate and Eastern. There was nothing on the stage itself except the grain jar, which we placed toward the back of the center of the stage, far enough away from the back wall so that we could put a little stool behind it, and so that the actors could walk and dance around it.

We played the magic scenes in front of the closed stage curtains, and lighted this area with a floodlight from the side of the audience. During these scenes, the Potted Princess had time to stand up and stretch!

In another production, when we did not have a stage curtain, we had our Two Servants bring a screen onto the stage and place it in front of the grain jar for the magic scenes. The Servants stood at attention at each side of the screen to hold it. The first magic scene was a green, shadowy, woodsy spot painted on an old sheet which was tacked to the top of the screen. After the Gnome scene, the Servants flipped another sheet, which had been hanging down the back of the screen, over the first one. This one was painted like a cloud-castle for the Fairy Queen. After this scene, both of these sheets were flipped to the back of the screen to show the screen itself painted to look like a World's End of swirly, smoky, lightning-streaked sky, for the Witch. After the Witch scene, the Servants took the screen off stage and the stage again became the courtyard with the Potted Princess in the grain jar.

Another time, we used this same idea of screen scenery for the magic scenes, but put the screen on a separate platform at the side of the stage and lighted it with a floodlight.

To make the magic scenes seem far apart and far away, each Magic Creature came from the back of the audience to his own particular music. Each Prince galloped on and off around the audience to the sound of music and hoofbeats. To make the hoofbeats, an actor in the back of the audience clapped his cupped hands on his thighs in gallop rhythm.

We selected music which would help the different moods of the play. We wanted court music which would be right for an Oriental fairy tale. For this we chose records from *The Nutcracker Suite* by Tchaikovsky. The *Arab Dance* was the theme for the entrance of all the court characters, and for the Princess's dance. From this same symphony, we used the *Prince and Princess* for a theme when the Son of the Potter was acting.

Since magic is not of any period, we chose music of the magic scenes and for the magic dances at the court to fit each special Magic Creature. The quick, hoppy, choppy rhythm of Prokofiev's *Parade of the Grasshoppers* was good for our Gnome. The calm, sweet melody of Prokofiev's *Evening* was right for our graceful, dreamy Fairy Queen; and the clashing ending of the Tchaikovsky *Symphony Number Four*, accompanied by thunder and lightning, was an exciting background for Old Mother Witch. To make the sound of thunder, we rattled a sheet of tin which hung off stage and added extra noise by striking an iron skillet with a mallet so that it sounded like a reverberating gong.

Our grain jar was a big wooden barrel painted to look like red clay. We bored some air holes in the back of it. The lid was made out of an old umbrella top covered with brown paper and painted to match the barrel. Inside the barrel was a small stool for the Princess to climb down onto and then sit on. She climbed into the barrel from another small stool behind it.

We borrowed real Oriental drums for our Two Servants to beat. Children's toy drums, or pans, covered with cloth and painted with Oriental designs, could be used. Oriental drums are beaten by striking them with the palm of your hand.

Our Witch's cauldron was a black iron pot. We lighted incense inside it for smoke.

To make a toadstool big enough for our Gnome to get under, and lightweight enough for her to carry easily, we covered a big umbrella with brown paper and painted on it red and yellow dots. If you want to have a substantial toadstool or mushroom which you can sit on, stand a stick of round firewood on end and turn a big wooden salad bowl upside down on top of it. You do not need to attach the top, so Mother can have the salad bowl back!

Use a necklace that will not break. We painted wooden beads green, sprinkled them with glitter, and strung them on a heavy green cord.

To make our scales of shiny fish, we threaded many oval bits of cellophane together.

The shield was a cardboard cutout covered with aluminum foil.

The Fairy Queen wore garlands of paper flowers. One string of them had many little paper blossoms which she pulled off and scattered over the grain jar when she danced her magic dance.

The crystal ball of the Wisemen was a glass fish bowl.

In costuming this play, we studied illustrations from the stories in the *Arabian Nights*. Then we started a treasure hunt for flowing silk pajamas. The Princess, Queen and Potter's Wife sewed elastic in the bottoms of their pajama pants, to blouse them at the ankles. The King, Servants, Princes and Potter's Son tucked theirs to blouse over sock-boots. Pajama tops were belted in with wide flowing sashes of different colors. Headpieces were colored scarves wound around in turban style, or fastened tight across the forehead and hanging loose at the sides and back of the head.

The Princess wore loose flowing veiling over her pajamas, scarves hanging from a jeweled headband, and many jewels. The Wisemen wore bathrobes with long sashes. They tied white mop beards over their ears. Their turbans were made of striped bath towels.

Socks or ballet slippers with pointed cutouts of cardboard attached for curved toes were good footgear.

Crowns were made of corrugated cardboard covered with foil and decorated with jewels and beads.

We wanted our Witch to have a costume which would flutter and swirl when she moved. So we sewed long fringed pieces of black silk to the shoulders of a black cape. She wore this cape over a black shirt and full black skirt to which we glued some glitter designs. We sewed long strands of rope hair to her conical hat.

Our Gnome wore a green leotard. We glued gold glitter to it and made a tiny pair of gold-foil wings to safety-pin to her back. Her little felt cap was covered with gold foil. She was a very pretty little creature. You could make a weird, ugly Gnome by fastening a clothes hanger upside down across the back of the Gnome's shoulders and padding it with toweling before he pulls on his costume. Add a wispy yarn beard and thick pointed eyebrows.

Our Fairy Queen wore a yellow leotard, over which were hung filmy fringed scarves of pastel nylon. On her costume were butterflies and flowers made of crepe paper and glitter. Glitter was glued to her silver wand. Her headband was jeweled. Her wings were long scarves pinned together at the back of her costume and attached to her wrists, so the filmy scarves fluttered as she waved her arms. These are the best kinds of wings for all creatures who want to flutter softly—for instance, angels and butterflies. Use thin material which is long enough to reach from wrist to wrist of your actor's outstretched arms. You can fringe the bottom edge of the material, or cut it into a curved or scalloped shape. To make a lovely butterfly, you can use several different colors of scarves or pieces of thin silk or net or veiling. Paint butterfly markings on the top one. Pile them on top of each other, gather them up, and sew them together in the center. Fasten wrist elastics to the top corners of the wings. Safety-pin the wings where they have been sewn together to the back of a yellow, green, blue or purple leotard or bathing suit. To your butterfly's little cap, sew pipe-cleaner antennae.

THE MAGIC FISHBONE

THE MAGIC FISHBONE

(A Romance from the Pen of Miss Alice Rainbird, Aged Seven)

A dramatization based on the story by Charles Dickens

CHARACTERS

KING WATKINS THE FIRST

HIS QUEEN

ALICIA, THEIR ELDEST DAUGHTER

HER TEN BROTHERS AND SISTERS

THE FAIRY GRANDMARINA

PRINCE CERTAINPERSONIO

The play takes place in the home of KING WATKINS THE FIRST. *We see a big room which is rather shabby, for the royal family is in the midst of hard times. The stage is quite bare. There is a big fireplace at the right end and a bed at the left end. Along the entire back wall of the room runs a long shelf on which are wooden bowls, spoons, containers of soup ingredients, cooks' hats. At the right end of the shelf are basin, smelling bottle, sponge. At the left end of the shelf, ragbag, scissors, needle and thread, flatiron. There is a small stool in front of the fireplace and a big black kettle inside the fireplace. A pianist, off stage, is playing the nursery rhyme music of* To Market, To Market *as the curtain opens. The royal family is on the stage standing posed like a picture. The* CHILDREN *are lined up according to size in front of the shelf, with* ALICIA *at the left end of the line-up. The* QUEEN *stands in front of the fireplace, facing the* KING *who stands at the other end of the room in front of the bed. Everyone stands rigid, with hands carefully folded in front of him. When the* QUEEN *speaks and breaks the spell, the* CHILDREN *turn their heads to listen to her.*

QUEEN. Say good-by to your father now. He is going to his office.

CHILDREN (*turn heads to* KING). Good-by, Papa.

KING (*shakes his head sadly*). You all seem to be growing out of your clothes. I wish it were quarter day so I could receive my salary!

QUEEN. They are indeed growing out of their clothes, my dear. Quarter days are so far apart, aren't they? But we are all happy and healthy, at any rate, aren't we, my loves?

CHILDREN (*turn heads to* QUEEN). Oh yes, Mama. We are growing out of our clothes but we are all happy and healthy.

(*The* KING *moves along the line of* CHILDREN *quickly, kissing each one. Then he kisses the* QUEEN. *The music accompanies his action by playing quickly down the scale.*)

QUEEN. And, my dear, don't forget to stop at the fishmonger's and buy a pound and a half of salmon not too near the tail.

KING. Yes, my dear. I have just enough pocket money left for that. (*He crosses back to stage left, turns and waves.*) Good-by.

CHILDREN (*turn to him and wave*). Good-by, Papa.

(*The* KING *leaves the stage and comes into the auditorium as the curtains close behind him. To the musical accompaniment of* To Market, To Market, *he jogs down the aisle of the audience and circles back in front of the stage. He has picked up a package of fish en route. When he is in front of the stage, the lights flicker, the music changes to magic music of* The Man in the Moon, *and there by the* KING *is the* FAIRY GRANDMARINA.)

FAIRY GRANDMARINA. King Watkins the First, I believe?

KING (*bows*). Watkins is my name.

FAIRY GRANDMARINA. Papa, if I am not mistaken, of the beautiful Princess Alicia?

KING. And of ten other little darlings.

FAIRY GRANDMARINA. I am the good Fairy Grandmarina. Attend! When you return home to dinner, politely invite the Princess Alicia to have some of the salmon you bought just now.

KING. It may disagree with her.

FAIRY GRANDMARINA (*stamps her foot angrily*). We hear a great deal too much about this thing disagreeing and that thing disagreeing. Don't be greedy. I think you want it all yourself.

KING (*bows humbly*). I beg your pardon. I'll never say such a thing again.

FAIRY GRANDMARINA. Be good, then, and don't! When the beautiful Princess Alicia consents to partake of the salmon—as I think she will—you will find she will leave a fishbone on her plate. Tell her to dry it, and to rub it, and to polish it, till it shines like mother-of-pearl, and to take care of it as a present from me.

KING. Is that all?

FAIRY GRANDMARINA (*scolds*). Don't be impatient, sir. Don't catch people short before they have done speaking. Just the way with you grown-up persons. You are always doing it.

KING (*hangs his head*). I beg your pardon. I won't do it again.

FAIRY GRANDMARINA. Be good, then, and don't! Tell the Princess Alicia, with my love, that the fishbone is a magic present which can only be used once; but that it will bring her, that once, whatever she wishes for, PROVIDED SHE WISHES FOR IT AT THE RIGHT TIME. That is the message. Take care of it.

KING. Might I ask the reason?

FAIRY GRANDMARINA (*stamps furiously*). WILL you be good, sir? The reason for this, and the reason for that, indeed! You are always wanting the reason. No reason. There! Hoity-toity me! I am sick of your grown-up reasons.

KING (*frightened*). I'm sorry to have offended you. I won't ask for reasons any more.

FAIRY GRANDMARINA. Be good, then, and don't! (*Lights flicker, magic music, and she vanishes.*)

KING. Where did she go? (*He parts the stage curtains and disappears behind them.*)

(*To the music of* Polly Put the Kettle On, *the curtains open on the same scene with which we started.*)

KING. And now, my dear Alicia, you must dry the fishbone, and rub it, and polish it, till it shines like mother-of-pearl.

CHILDREN. (*They look at Alicia as she dries the fishbone on her apron, rubs it, and polishes it.*) You must dry the fishbone, and rub it, and polish it, till it shines like mother-of-pearl.

KING. It is a magic present which can only be used once; and it will bring you, she said, that once, whatever you wish for, provided you wish for it at the right time. That is the message.

QUEEN. (*She runs across the stage and falls upon the couch, as the music plays tiny little scales.*) Oh, dear me, dear me, my head, my head! (*She faints.*)

ALICIA (*kneels beside her mother*). Oh, my dear royal Mama. You have fainted dead away!

CHILDREN. (*They face their Mama, hands raised in dismay.*) Oh, my dear royal Mama. You have fainted dead away! (*pause*) Alicia, use your fishbone to make our royal Mama well!

ALICIA. First, get me the smelling bottle.

LITTLEST ONE (*whirls around and gets the smelling bottle*). Smelling bottle! (*She passes it to the child beside her.*)

EACH CHILD (*passing the bottle quickly down the line*). Smelling bottle!

ALICIA (*takes bottle and holds it to Mama's nose*). Get me some water!

LITTLEST ONE (*whirls around and gets the basin*). Water! (*She passes the basin to the* CHILD *beside her.*)

EACH CHILD (*passing the basin quickly down the line*). Water!

ALICIA (*takes the basin*). Get me a sponge.

LITTLEST ONE (*whirls around and gets the sponge*). Sponge! (*She passes the sponge to the child beside her.*)

EACH CHILD (*passing the sponge quickly down the line*). Sponge!

ALICIA (*She hands the basin to the* KING *to hold, as she applies the sponge to the* QUEEN's *forehead.*) She is better, I think. Now Papa, you watch her, while I put the children to bed.

(*As the music plays* Bye, Baby Bunting, ALICIA *tiptoes down the row of* CHILDREN. *As she hushes each* CHILD, *he leans his head to the left on his hands and goes to sleep.*)

KING (*beckons to* ALICIA *and whispers*). Alicia!

ALICIA (*going back to him*). Yes, Papa.

KING. What has become of the magic fishbone?

ALICIA. In my pocket, Papa!

KING. I thought you had lost it!

ALICIA. Oh, no, Papa!

KING. Or forgotten it?

ALICIA. No, indeed, Papa.

NEXT TO LITTLEST CHILD (*who has sneaked off the stage, now enters*). OOOOOOOOOOOOH!

· 87 ·

CHILDREN (*wake up, raise their hands*). OOOOOOOOOOH! (*They scream this up the scale and hold it there on their breath.*)

NEXT TO LITTLEST CHILD. That little pug dog next door rushed at me and in my hurry to get in the house, I put my hand through a pane of glass.

CHILDREN (*wailing down the scale*). OOOOOOOOOOOOH!

ALICIA (*rushes down the row of* CHILDREN, *quieting them*). Hush-sh-sh-sh-sh-sh-sh-sh-sh-sh! (*She sits on the stool by the fireplace and looks at the injured hand of the* NEXT TO LITTLEST CHILD.) Get me a basin of fresh cold water!

NEXT TO OLDEST CHILD (*whirls around and gets the basin from the* KING). Water! (*She passes it quickly to the* CHILD *beside her.*)

EACH CHILD (*passing the basin quickly down the line*). Water!

ALICIA (*holds the basin*). There, there, put your hand in this. Now I will see if there are any bits of glass in your hand. Get me the royal ragbag.

NEXT TO OLDEST CHILD (*whirls around and gets the ragbag*). Ragbag! (*She passes it quickly to the* CHILD *beside her.*)

EACH CHILD (*passing the ragbag quickly down the line*). Ragbag!

ALICIA (*finds a bit of cloth*). Bring me a large pair of scissors!

NEXT TO OLDEST CHILD (*whirls around and gets the scissors*). Scissors! (*She passes them quickly to the* CHILD *beside her.*)

EACH CHILD (*passing the scissors quickly down the line*). Scissors!

ALICIA (*cuts a bandage*). Bring me a needle and thread.

NEXT TO OLDEST CHILD (*whirls around and gets a needle and*

thread). Needle and thread! (*She passes it quickly to the* CHILD *beside her.*)

EACH CHILD (*passing the needle and thread quickly down the line*). Needle and thread!

ALICIA (*completes the bandage*). There it fits beautifully!

CHILDREN (*watching her*). It fits beautifully!

KING (*who has stood helplessly near the* QUEEN's *bed*). Alicia!

ALICIA (*puts the* NEXT TO LITTLEST CHILD *back in her place in the row of* CHILDREN *and goes to the* KING). Yes, Papa.

KING. What have you been doing?

ALICIA. Snipping, stitching, cutting and contriving, Papa.

KING. Where is the magic fishbone?

ALICIA. In my pocket, Papa.

KING. I thought you had lost it.

ALICIA. Oh, no, Papa.

KING. Or forgotten it?

ALICIA. No, indeed, Papa.

LITTLEST ONE (*falls into the fireplace*). OOOOOOOOOOH!

CHILDREN. (*They look at the* LITTLEST ONE, *with their hands raised in fright.*) The Littlest One has fallen in the fire!

ALICIA. (*She rushes down the row of* CHILDREN *hushing them.*) Hold your tongues, you wicked little monkeys, every one of you or you will make our royal Mama worse. I will examine the Littlest One.

CHILDREN. Has he broken himself?

ALICIA. (*She sits on the stool and takes the* LITTLEST ONE *on her knee.*) He has not broken anything. Bring me a cold iron.

NEXT TO OLDEST CHILD (*whirls around and gets an iron*). Cold iron! (*She passes it quickly to the* CHILD *beside her.*)

EACH CHILD (*passing the iron quickly down the line*). Cold iron!

ALICIA. I will hold it to his poor dear eye. There! I think he will go to sleep.

CHILDREN (*sing while* ALICIA *rocks the* LITTLEST ONE. CHILDREN *rock their arms as a cradle*). Bye, Baby Bunting.

ALICIA (*after they have finished the lullaby*). I am afraid to let him down yet, lest he should wake and feel pain; be good, and you shall all be cooks.

CHILDREN (*jump joyfully*). Hurrah, we shall all be cooks.

ALICIA. Put on your cook hats.

(*Each* CHILD *whirls around, picks up his cook hat, puts it on, and faces front.*)

NEXT TO OLDEST CHILD. I will get the salt. (*She whirls around and picks up her container of salt and faces front.*)

NEXT CHILD. I will get the barley. (*same action*)

NEXT CHILD. I will get the herbs. (*same action*)

NEXT CHILD. I will get the turnips. (*same action*)

NEXT CHILD. I will get the carrots. (*same action*)

NEXT CHILD. I will get the onions. (*same action*)

NEXT CHILD. I will get the spice box. (*same action*)

NEXT CHILD. I will get the potatoes. (*same action*)

NEXT CHILD. I will get the soup bone. (*same action*)

(*Now they are all facing the front with their cook hats on. Each* CHILD *holds his container of ingredients. To the music of* Polly Put the Kettle On, *they march, following*

*the leader across to the fireplace, empty ingredients into
the big kettle, and prance back to their places.)*

ALICIA. (*She takes the* LITTLEST ONE *to the center of the stage
and puts him on the floor.*) Laugh and be good. And you
may sit here on the floor and after dinner you will see a dance
of the cooks. (*She goes to the kettle.*) The broth is done. Get
your bowls.

(The CHILDREN *whirl around, put their containers down
on the shelf and pick up their bowls and spoons and face
front again. The* KING *also gets a bowl and spoon. To
the music of* Hot Cross Buns, *the* CHILDREN, *led by the*
KING, *march to the fireplace where* ALICIA *dishes the soup.
Then they march back to their line-up.* ALICIA *takes a bowl
and sits by the* LITTLEST ONE *in the center of the stage.)*

ALL (*smelling the soup*). It smells so good!

*(To the music, they eat their soup, and then whirl around
to put their bowls back on the shelf. Then, led by the* KING,
they dance around ALICIA *and the* LITTLEST ONE. *As the
music changes to* Bye, Baby Bunting, *the* CHILDREN *return to their line-up, close their eyes, and lean their heads
on their hands.* ALICIA *puts the* LITTLEST ONE *back in his
place in the line.)*

KING. Alicia.

ALICIA. (*goes to him*). Yes, Papa.

KING. Where is the magic fishbone, Alicia?

ALICIA. In my pocket, Papa.

KING. I thought you had lost it.

ALICIA. Oh, no, Papa!

KING. Or forgotten it?

ALICIA. No, indeed, Papa.

KING. (*He walks slowly to the center of the stage and sits on the floor. He sighs heavily*) Oh dear! (*puts his head in his hands*)

ALICIA (*comes to him*). What is the matter, Papa?

KING. I am dreadfully poor, my child.

ALICIA. Have you no money at all, Papa?

KING. None, my child.

ALICIA. Is there no way of getting any, Papa?

KING. No way. I have tried very hard, and tried all ways.

ALICIA. Papa, when we have tried very hard, and tried all ways, we must have done our very, very best?

KING. No doubt, Alicia.

ALICIA. When we have done our very, very best, Papa, and that is not enough, then I think the right time must have come for asking help of others. (*takes the fishbone out of her pocket and kisses it, holds it up high, looks straight ahead of her, and says slowly*) I wish it were quarter day!

> (*The lights flicker, the music is magic. Down the chimney rattle many gold pieces and pour onto the floor. The* CHILDREN *and the* QUEEN *wake up, jump up and down, dance over to the fireplace, and pick up the gold coins as the music plays excitedly. When they have returned to their places with their coins, out of the fireplace steps the* FAIRY GRANDMARINA.)

FAIRY GRANDMARINA. Alicia, my dear, how do you do? I hope I see you pretty well. Give me a kiss. (*They embrace at stage center.*)

FAIRY GRANDMARINA (*turns to the* KING, *who is now standing in front of the bed with his arm around his happy* QUEEN) Are you good?

KING (*bows low*). I hope so.

FAIRY GRANDMARINA. I suppose you know the reason NOW why my goddaughter here did not apply to the fishbone sooner?

KING (*bows again shyly*). I do so.

FAIRY GRANDMARINA. Ah! but you didn't THEN?

KING (*bows ever more shyly*). No, I'm afraid not.

FAIRY GRANDMARINA. Any more reasons to ask for?

KING. No more reasons. I am very sorry not to have known.

FAIRY GRANDMARINA. Be good, then, and live happy ever afterwards. (*She waves her fan. The lights flash, the magic music plays.*)

> (*While the lights are flashing, the* CHILDREN *dance off the stage and into the audience. At the back of the audience, each child takes off his smock, circles around and back to the stage dressed in the most beautiful costume. Meantime, on stage, the* FAIRY GRANDMARINA *has tapped the* KING *and* QUEEN *with her fan. Their old robes drop off, and they are costumed in royal finery. As the* CHILDREN *dance back to their places, the* FAIRY GRANDMARINA *is helping* ALICIA *place a bridal veil on her head. For* ALICIA's *old apron has disappeared, and* ALICIA *is wearing a wedding dress.*)

FAIRY GRANDMARINA. Now all we need is Prince Certainpersonio. (*She waves her fan.*) Ah! here he comes. (*A little boy wanders in.*) Prince, here is your bride. (*She taps him with her wand, and his clothes are velvet; a cap and feather complete his Princely attire.*)

PRINCE CERTAINPERSONIO. This must be my Princess Alicia! (*bows and kisses her hand*)

ALICIA (*bows*). And you are Prince Certainpersonio.

FAIRY GRANDMARINA. Now we will all go to the church. And after you are married, we will have a great feast.

CHILDREN (*clap their hands and then hold them high*). Hip, hip, hip, hurrah!

FAIRY GRANDMARINA. And in the future there will be eight quarter days in every year, except in leap year, when there will be ten.

CHILDREN (*same action*). Hip, hip, hip, hurrah!

FAIRY GRANDMARINA. And you will have thirty-five children, and they will all be good and beautiful. Seventeen of your children will be boys, and eighteen will be girls. The hair of the whole of your children will curl naturally. They will never have the measles, and will have recovered from the whooping cough before being born.

CHILDREN (*same action*). Hip, hip, hip, hurrah!

FAIRY GRANDMARINA. In conclusion, it only remains to make an end of the fishbone.

(*The fishbone, at a wave from the fan, flies across the stage and up out of sight. Everyone points to it in wonder, as the* CURTAIN *closes.*)

PRODUCTION NOTES

Charles Dickens, who wrote this fairy tale, pretended that it was written by a seven-year-old girl named Alice Rainbird. Alice Rainbird made her King and Queen and their many children like the families she knew in her own time in England. They worried about Papa's salary, and whether it would last from one payday to the next when there were so many children to feed and clothe. They didn't have servants; the oldest daughter, Alicia, took care of the younger children. The Fairy was much more like a real grandmother than like a fairy-tale fairy. She had a fan instead of a wand. She was very cross with adults who asked unnecessary questions and wanted reasons for everything. Her magic present was an ordinary fishbone instead of some mysterious wishing stone. The things that Alicia had to take care of were the kinds of upsets and accidents that might happen in any large family. Mama got sick, one child hurt his hand, another fell into the fireplace. Alicia took care of all these things in a common-sense way. She saved her magic fishbone to help her Papa when she could not find an ordinary way to manage.

So we decided to play the story just as if the King and Queen and Princes and Princesses were an ordinary family, except that they wore crowns.

Our stage looked like an ordinary room, except that on the wall was the royal coat of arms of King Watkins the First. We hinged together our six screens painted like brown wood paneling to make the back of the room. At the end of the stage on the left we made an enormous fireplace out of painted cardboard boxes.

At the other end of the room we put a bench bed. Since all of the big family were always on the stage, we had to decide how to work out the action so that it would be clear and not all cluttered up. We decided to have the children do the same things at the same time and make their actions and speech rather like puppets. This kind of acting is called "stylization," because instead of acting naturally everyone acts in a certain set style, or pattern. We lined the children up according to size across the back of the stage. Each one had his place in the line-up. Their gestures and movements were almost like a ballet. When they marched and danced, they did it in a follow-the-leader pattern, so that the action was always clear. Since the children, except for Alicia, had very few lines, this pattern to their gestures and actions and speech was amusing. But it needed a lot of practice to make it good. Much of the action was put to music to help set the different patterns of action. We thought nursery rhyme music fitted this kind of play best.

Because we needed a place for each child to have his props,

we put a long narrow shelf against the back wall. We made this out of cardboard boxes the same size, set on end. On this shelf behind each child were the things he would need to use in the play. He could get them easily and quickly by simply turning around in his place. We worked out the turns so that they too were patterned.

The props were "stylized," too, so they would fit the whole idea of the play. The soup ingredients were simply cardboard boxes all painted alike except for the lettering on each: "Spice Box," "Onions," etc. Each child made his own cook hat out of newspaper. The hats fitted over their little crowns.

The gold coins were cardboard circles covered with gold foil. The actors started making these at the first rehearsals, so we could have lots and lots of them. Anyone who was not busy acting was making gold coins. We put them in a big paper bag behind the fireplace, so that at the proper time an actor off stage could empty the coins down the chimney. At the same time this actor shook a chain of brass curtain rings, to make a noise of the money falling.

The fishbone was a small forked stick with a rubber band around it. We rigged a fishline from behind the fireplace to the top of the stage through screw eyes. We tied a safety pin to the end of the line and pinned this at the back of the stage, as high as an actor could reach. This line was invisible from the audience. While the magic scene of making Alicia into a bride was happening in the middle of the stage, an actor got the fishbone from Alicia's apron pocket, unpinned the line, and pinned the safety pin through the rubber band on the fishbone. At the right moment for the fishbone to fly away, the actor behind the fireplace pulled the fishline rigging, and the fishbone flew through the air and up behind the border at the front of the stage.

The appearing and disappearing of the Fairy was done simply by flickering the lights and playing magic music as she ran on and off.

A big problem was the changing of the clothing. We solved

this by having each little Princess wear her best party dress with pantalets. Over the dress she wore a smock. The boys wore knee pants and fancy blouses, with smocks over them. The children took off the smocks when they danced around the audience. The Queen wore a long dressing gown over her gorgeous queen costume. The King wore a long coat over his royal finery. Alicia wore an enormous apron over her bridal dress. Her veil was in the apron pocket. The Fairy Grandmarina wore a silk and lace skirt, a blouse and bonnet. The old illustrations of F. D. Bedford in the edition published by Frederick Warne & Co., Ltd., gave us some good ideas. There are also charming illustrations by Louis Slobodkin in the 1953 Vanguard Press edition.

Because we stylized this play, it was easy to do as far as the words of the play were concerned. But it took a lot of real work to get the action and the picture to be clever and gay. The group acting, which is the most important part of all our plays, was especially important in this one.

You might want to do this play in an entirely different way by working out the lines and action realistically, instead of by a pattern of artificial style. In a bigger production, the scene at Mr. Pickles', the fishmonger, could be added. Perhaps some groups could figure out how to do the carriage drawn by peacocks. Or you might want to include the scenes where Alicia talks with her doll, the duchess. The play could have a larger or smaller cast by changing the number of little Princesses and Princes. Read the story by Dickens and decide how to adapt it to your own needs.

Because the part of Prince Certainpersonio was so small, and came at the end of the play, he was our stage manager and worked the lights, sound effects and fireplace money. In the next play, of course, he had a long part.

THE RELUCTANT DRAGON

THE RELUCTANT DRAGON

A dramatization based on the story by Kenneth Grahame
found in his book *Dream Days,* John Lane, 1898, London.

CHARACTERS

BOY

HIS MOTHER

HIS FATHER

THE HEAD OF THE RELUCTANT DRAGON

HIS LEFT PAW

HIS RIGHT PAW

HIS TAIL

EIGHT VILLAGERS

ST. GEORGE

*The play takes place Long Ago in the shepherd country of Eng-
land. At the back right corner of the stage is a screen painted
to look like rough boards. This is the cottage where the* BOY
*lives. Later in the play, it is the Village Inn. The rest of the
stage is open countryside with blue sky, a few bushes and rocks,
a wind-blown tree. At stage left is the rocky entrance to an
enormous cave. This side of the stage is very dim, but there is
bright light on the cottage where the* BOY *sits on a little stool
reading a big book and his* MOTHER *sits on a little stool sewing.
After a bit of homey quiet, the* FATHER *rushes onto the stage
from off right.*

FATHER (*shaking with fear*). It's all up with me, Maria! Never
no more can I go up on them there Downs, be it ever so!

MOTHER (*calmly*). Now don't you take on like that, but tell us
all about it first, whatever it is as has given you this shake-up,

and then me and you and the Son here, between us, we ought to be able to get to the bottom of it!

FATHER. It began some nights ago. You know that cave up there—I never liked it somehow, and the sheep never liked it neither, and when sheep don't like a thing there is generally some reason for it. Well, for some time past there's been faint noises coming from that cave—noises like heavy sighings, with grunts mixed up in them; and sometimes a snoring, far away down—*real* snoring, yet somehow not *honest* snoring, like you and me o' nights, you know!

BOY (*quietly*). I know.

FATHER. Of course I was terrible frightened; yet somehow I couldn't keep away. So this very evening, before I come down, I took a cast round by the cave, quietly. And there— O Lord, there I saw him at last, as plain as I see you!

MOTHER. Saw WHO?

FATHER. Why HIM, I'm a-telling you! He was sticking halfway out of the cave and seemed to be enjoying of the cool of the evening in a poetical sort of way. He was big as four cart horses, and all covered with shiny scales. He had his chin on his paws, and I should say he was meditating about things. Oh yes, a peaceable sort o' beast enough, and not ramping or carrying on or doing anything but what was quite right and proper. I admit all that. And yet, what am I to do? SCALES, you know, and claws, and a tail for certain, though I didn't see that end of him—I ain't USED to 'em, and I don't HOLD with 'em, and that's a fact!

BOY (*closes his book, yawns, clasps his hands behind his head*). It's all right, Father. Don't you worry. It's only a Dragon.

FATHER. Only a Dragon? What do you mean, sitting there, you and your Dragons? ONLY a Dragon indeed! And what do YOU know about it?

BOY (*quietly*). 'Cos it IS, and 'cos I DO know. Look here, Father, you know we've each of us got our line. *You* know about sheep and weather and things; *I* know about Dragons. I always said, you know, that that cave up there was a Dragon-cave. Now please, just leave this all to me. I'll go up and have a talk to him, and you'll find it'll be all right. Only, please don't you go worrying round there without me. You don't understand 'em a bit, and they're very sensitive, you know!

MOTHER. He's quite right, Father. As he says, Dragons is his line and not ours. He's wonderful knowing about book-beasts, as everyone allows. And to tell the truth, I'm not half happy in my own mind, thinking of that poor animal lying alone up there, without a bit o' hot supper or anyone to change the news with; and if he ain't quite respectable our Boy'll find it out quick enough. He's got a pleasant sort o' way with him that makes everybody tell him everything. Now, you two come along to bed now! (*She leads the* BOY *off right, followed by the* FATHER.)

(*The lights dim on the cottage and brighten on the cave entrance. The* DRAGON *emerges from his cave, looks happily about him, puts his chin on his paws, and purrs blissfully. The* BOY *enters from stage right.*)

BOY. Well, we live and learn! None of my books ever told me that Dragons purred! (*Goes nearer*) Hallo, Dragon!

DRAGON HEAD (*severely*). Now don't you hit me, or bung stones, or squirt water, or anything. I won't have it, I tell you!

BOY (*calmly*). I've simply looked in to ask you how you were and all that sort of thing; but if I'm in the way I can easily clear out.

DRAGON LEFT PAW. No, no, don't go off in a huff. Fact is—I'm as happy up here as the day's long; never without an occupation, dear fellow, never without an occupation! And yet, between ourselves, it *is* a trifle dull at times.

BOY (*politely*). Going to make a long stay here?

DRAGON RIGHT PAW. Can't hardly say at present. It seems a nice place enough; but I've only been here a short time, and one must look about and reflect and consider before settling down. Besides—fact is, I'm such a confounded lazy beggar!

BOY. You surprise me.

DRAGON TAIL. It's the sad truth; and I fancy that's really how I came to be here. You see all the other fellows were so active and EARNEST and all that sort of thing—always rampaging, and skirmishing, and scouring the desert sands, and pacing the margin of the sea, and chasing knights all over the place, and devouring damsels—whereas I liked to get my meals regular and then to prop my back against a bit of rock and snooze a bit, and wake up and think of things going on and how they kept going on just the same, you know! So when it happened I got fairly caught.

BOY. When *what* happened, please?

DRAGON HEAD. That's just what I don't precisely know. I suppose the earth sneezed, or shook itself, or the bottom dropped out of something. Anyhow there was a shake and a roar and a general stramash, and I found myself miles away underground and wedged in as tight as tight. Well, thank goodness, my wants are few, and I had peace and quiet. But time went on, and there was a certain sameness about the life, and at last I began to think it would be fun to work my way upstairs and see what the other fellows were doing. So I scratched and burrowed, and at last I came out through this cave here. On the whole I feel inclined to settle down here.

BOY. What's your mind always occupied about?

DRAGON LEFT PAW (*bashfully*). Did you ever—just for fun—try to make up poetry—verses, you know?

BOY. 'Course I have. Heaps of it. And some of it's quite good, I feel sure, only there's no one here cares about it. . . .

DRAGON RIGHT PAW. Exactly; my own case exactly. Now you've got culture, you have, I could tell it on you at once. I'm awfully pleased to have met you, and I'm hoping the other neighbors will be equally agreeable. There was a very nice old gentleman up here only last night, but he didn't seem to want to intrude.

BOY. That was my Father, and he IS a nice old gentleman, and I'll introduce you some day if you like.

DRAGON TAIL (*eagerly*). Can't you two come up here and dine tomorrow?

BOY. Thanks awfully, but we don't go out anywhere without my Mother, and, to tell you the truth, I'm afraid she mightn't quite approve of you. You see, there's no getting over the hard fact that you're a Dragon, is there? And when you talk of settling down, I can't help feeling that you don't quite realize your position. You're an enemy of the human race, you see!

DRAGON HEAD (*cheerfully*). Haven't got an enemy in the world. Too lazy to make 'em, to begin with.

BOY. Oh, dear! I wish you'd try and grasp the situation properly. When the other people find you out, they'll come after you with spears and swords and all sorts of things. You'll have to be exterminated, according to their way of looking at it! You're a scourge, and a pest, and a baneful monster!

DRAGON LEFT PAW. Not a word of truth in it. Character'll bear the strictest investigation. And now, there's a little sonnet-thing I was working on. . . .

BOY. I can't stop for sonnets. Do for goodness' sake try and realize that you're a pestilential scourge, or you'll find yourself in a most awful fix. Good night! (*The* BOY *waves good-*

by as he goes off the stage. The DRAGON *waves, yawns, and backs carefully into his cave, as the lights dim.)*

(After a few moments of quiet, which mean the night has passed, the right side of the stage brightens. From different parts of the audience the VILLAGERS *come singing to the stage. They carry small stools and beer mugs. They greet each other and settle themselves on their stools in a half circle at stage right.)*

VILLAGERS (*singing*). I am athirst, what should I say?
          Alas! I have no money to pay.
          Fill the pot, Butler, fill, fill,
          For I will drink with a good will.

FIRST VILLAGER (*after the singing stops*). I say he's a pestilential scourge!

SECOND VILLAGER. Fancy! A real live Dragon in the cave on our Downs!

THIRD VILLAGER. Just where we were a-picnicking, peaceful as could be, only last Sunday!

FOURTH VILLAGER. As big as four cart horses!

FIFTH VILLAGER. And covered from tip to tail with SCALES!

SIXTH VILLAGER. In a way it's a distinction for a village to have a Dragon of its very own!

SEVENTH VILLAGER. Not many a village can say the same, that's sure!

EIGHTH VILLAGER. He sits there so quiet, he don't behave like a Dragon. . . .

FIRST VILLAGER. Well, that's his own lookout! He IS a Dragon and no denying it!

SECOND VILLAGER. They do say there's a Princess in the cave waiting to be freed!

THIRD VILLAGER. And I do hear tell many a sheep's been stolen o' nights!

FOURTH VILLAGER. Not only SHEEP! Children too, who have wandered on the Downs alone, have not come back. . . .

FIFTH VILLAGER. Who's telling you this?

SIXTH VILLAGER. Never mind, who's a-telling! Anyone knows what a Dragon does!

SEVENTH VILLAGER. My great grampa had tales enough in HIS time. Anyone knows what a Dragon does!

EIGHTH VILLAGER. This sort of thing can't go on!

FIRST VILLAGER. The dreadful beast must be EXTERMI-NATED!

SECOND VILLAGER. The countryside must be freed from this pest!

THIRD VILLAGER. This terror! This destroying scourge!

FOURTH VILLAGER (*rises*). Who will take sword and spear and free our suffering village?

FIFTH VILLAGER (*rises*). And rescue the captive Princess?

SIXTH VILLAGER (*rises*). And win deathless fame?

SEVENTH VILLAGER (*rises*). Who?

EIGHTH VILLAGER (*rises*). Who? Who?

(*They look at each other in silence. There is a pause and then they all sit down again.*)

FOURTH VILLAGER (*looks straight out at the audience and then rises in great excitement*). It's all right! He's a-coming!!

ALL OTHERS. WHO'S a-coming??

FOURTH VILLAGER. Why, St. George, of course!

(*They see him striding through the audience. They stand on their stools and cheer.*)

ALL. St. George! St. George!! St. George!!!

FIRST VILLAGER. He's heard tell of our Dragon. . . .

SECOND VILLAGER. He's coming on purpose to slay the deadly beast . . .

THIRD VILLAGER. And free us from his horrid yoke!

FOURTH VILLAGER. Oh my! Won't there be a jolly fight!

FIFTH VILLAGER. It's all up, Dragon! He's coming! He's coming!

SIXTH VILLAGER. Now we'll have a real fight!

SEVENTH VILLAGER. Who'll give me odds on George!

EIGHTH VILLAGER. Let's have a good look at him first!

ALL (*make a path for St. George, as they cheer and wave*). Hail, St. George!

ST. GEORGE (*striding through the* VILLAGERS, *goes to the stool at the center of the half circle and mounts it. He silences the* VILLAGERS *with a wave of his hands.*) Dear friends, I have come to rid your village of the dreadful Dragon.

(*The* VILLAGERS *all cheer.*)

ST. GEORGE. Tell me the wrongs which you have suffered and which I will avenge.

(*There is an awkward silence, in which the* VILLAGERS *prod each other.*)

FIRST VILLAGER. Well, sheep have been disappearing . . .

SECOND VILLAGER. And children . . .

THIRD VILLAGER. And crops ravished . . .

FOURTH VILLAGER. And a Princess bound in the cave . . .

FIFTH VILLAGER. And folk being murdered all over the place . . .

SIXTH VILLAGER. And thieving and wrongdoing such as would shame your ears to hear and my lips to speak it.

SEVENTH VILLAGER. We daren't even go out of doors for fear of being snatched alive . . .

EIGHTH VILLAGER. Or burned to a crisp because of his scorching breath a-blowing on us—and a-making waste our countryside.

ST. GEORGE. All will be well now. Sleep tonight, and tomorrow I will slay your foe. But now, good night!

(*The* VILLAGERS *bow to him, and go off in groups. As they go they look back at him and make bets on the fight.* ST. GEORGE *watches them go. Then he sits wearily on the stool and puts his head in his hands.*)

BOY (*enters politely*). May I come in, St. George?

ST. GEORGE (*kindly*). Yes, come in, Boy. Another tale of misery and wrong, I fear me. Well, it shall soon be avenged.

BOY. Nothing of the sort. There's a misunderstanding somewhere, and I want to put it right. (*He moves a stool close to* ST. GEORGE *and sits beside him.*) The fact is, this is a GOOD Dragon. And a friend of mine. Nobody can help liking him when once they know him.

ST. GEORGE (*smiles*). I like a fellow who sticks up for his friends. But that's not the question. I've been listening to tales of murder, theft and wrong. This Dragon has to be speedily exterminated.

BOY (*impatiently*). Oh, you've been taking in all the yarns those fellows have been telling you. Our Villagers are the biggest storytellers in all the country round. All they want is a FIGHT. I came down the street just now, and they were betting six to four on the Dragon!

ST. GEORGE (*sadly*). Six to four on the Dragon! This is an evil

world, and sometimes I begin to think that all the wickedness is not entirely bottled up inside the Dragons. And yet
—may there not be, at this very moment, some princess
within yonder gloomy cavern?

BOY (*earnestly*). I assure you, St. George, there's nothing of
the sort at all. The Dragon's a real gentleman, every inch
of him.

ST. GEORGE. Well, perhaps I've misjudged the animal. But
what are we to do? Here are the Dragon and I, almost face
to face, each supposed to be thirsting for each other's blood.
I don't see any way out of it, exactly.

BOY. I suppose you couldn't be persuaded to go away quietly,
could you?

ST. GEORGE. Impossible, I fear. Quite against the rules. YOU
know that.

BOY. Well then, look here, would you mind strolling up with
me and seeing the Dragon and talking it over?

ST. GEORGE (*rises*). Well, it's *irregular*, but really it seems
about the most sensible thing to do. Perhaps there won't
have to be any fight after all.

BOY (*follows him off the stage*). Oh, but I hope there will,
though!

(*They circle through the audience and come onto the
stage again. The lights grow dim on the Inn side of stage
and become brighter on the cave.*)

BOY (*calls out*). I've brought a friend to see you, Dragon!

DRAGON HEAD (*coming out from the cave*). Very pleased to
make your acquaintance, sir. Charming weather we're having!

BOY. This is St. George. We've come up to talk things over

quietly, Dragon, and do let us have a little straight common sense.

DRAGON LEFT PAW (*nervously*). So glad to meet you, St. George. You've been a great traveler, I hear, and I've always been rather a stay-at-home. But if you're stopping here any time. . . .

ST. GEORGE (*shake hands with the* DRAGON). I think we'd better try to come to some understanding about this little affair of ours. Now don't you think that the simplest plan would be just to fight it out, and let the best man win? They're betting on you down in the village, but I don't mind that!

BOY (*delighted*). Oh, yes, DO, Dragon. It'll save such a lot of bother!

DRAGON RIGHT PAW. Believe me, St. George, there's nobody in the world I'd sooner oblige than you and this young gentleman here. But the whole thing's nonsense, and conventionality, and popular thick-headedness. There's absolutely nothing to fight about, from beginning to end. And anyhow I'm not going to, so that settles it!

ST. GEORGE. But suppose I make you?

DRAGON TAIL. You can't. I should only go into my cave and retire for a time down the hole I came up. And as soon as you'd gone away, why I'd come up again. For I tell you frankly, I like this place, and I'm going to stay here!

ST. GEORGE (*looks around him*). This would be a beautiful place for a fight. These great rolling Downs—and me in my golden armor showing up against your big, blue, scaly coils! Think what a picture it would make!

DRAGON HEAD. Now you're trying to get at me through my artistic sensibilities. But it won't work. Not but what it would make a very pretty picture, as you say.

BOY. You must see, Dragon, that there's got to be a fight of some sort, 'cos you can't want to have to go down that dirty old hole again and stop there till goodness knows when.

ST. GEORGE (*thoughtfully*). It might be arranged. I MUST spear you somewhere, of course, but I'm not bound to hurt you very much. (*He walks the length of the* DRAGON, *looking him over.*) There's such a lot of you that there must be a few SPARE places somewhere. (*He prods the* DRAGON *with his spear in several places. Each time, the* DRAGON *giggles.*) Here, for instance. Or here! Or here!

DRAGON LEFT PAW. You're tickling, George! Those places won't do at all.

ST. GEORGE. Let's try somewhere else, then. Here! (*points his spear at the back folds of the* DRAGON's *neck*) All these folds of thick skin. If I speared you here you'd never even know I'd done it!

DRAGON RIGHT PAW (*anxiously*). But are you sure you can hit the right place?

ST. GEORGE. Of course I am. You leave that to me!

DRAGON TAIL. It's just because I've GOT to leave it to you that I'm asking.

BOY. Look here, Dragon, I don't see quite where you come in! There's to be a fight, apparently, and you're to be licked; and what I want to know is, what are you going to get out of it?

DRAGON HEAD. St. George, just tell him, please—what will happen after I'm vanquished in the deadly combat?

ST. GEORGE. Well, according to the rules there'll be speeches and things, and I shall explain that you're converted, and see the error of your ways, and so on.

DRAGON LEFT PAW. Quite so. And then?

ST. GEORGE. Oh, and then—why, and then there will be the usual banquet, I suppose.

DRAGON RIGHT PAW. Exactly. And that's where *I* come in. I'm bored to death up here, and no one really appreciates me. I'm going into Society, I am, and you'll find I've got all the qualities to endear me to people! So now that's all settled. . . .

ST. GEORGE. Remember, you'll have to do your proper share of the fighting, Dragon! I mean ramping, and breathing fire, and so on!

DRAGON TAIL. I'll do the best I can. (*yawns*) And now, good night! (*He backs into his cave as the lights grow dim.*)

ST. GEORGE (*as he and the* BOY *leave*). I knew I had forgotten something. There ought to be a princess. Terror-stricken and chained to a rock, and all that sort of thing. Boy, can't you arrange a princess?

BOY (*yawns*). I'm tired to death, and I can't arrange a princess, or anything more at this time of night. And my Mother's sitting up, and DO stop asking me to arrange more things till tomorrow!

(*They are now off the stage and the lights have dimmed until the stage is in blackness, for the night has come. After a few moments, the light brightens.* VILLAGERS *enter from different places in the audience. They are calling out to each other as they come to the stage. They get the stools from the Inn and, as they call to each other in a holiday mood of festivity, they line them up across the back of the stage and stand on them to watch the fight.*)

FIRST VILLAGER. Six to four on the Dragon!

SECOND VILLAGER. Wait till we collect on you!

THIRD VILLAGER. Taken—and glad to!

FOURTH VILLAGER. I'll raise that!

FIFTH VILLAGER. Don't get too near that cave!

SIXTH VILLAGER. If the Dragon wins, he'll take us on next!

SEVENTH VILLAGER. IF he wins! Sure he'll win!

EIGHTH VILLAGER. Anyway, keep your distance!

(The BOY, with his MOTHER and FATHER, join the crowd at the right side of the stage. MOTHER and FATHER carry baskets of food.)

BOY. He's coming! He's coming!

ALL (cheer). St. George! St. George!

(ST. GEORGE, in all his splendor, strides down the center aisle of the audience. He comes to center stage and bows to the cheering crowd. Then he walks, magnificently, to stage far right and poses.)

ALL. Now then, Dragon!!

(The DRAGON, with great snorts and bellows, comes from his cave. He lashes his tail, claws the ground, and gives a good show of fierceness.)

ALL. OO-OO-OO! Oh, well done, Dragon! Well done!

(The DRAGON bows and poses, at stage left.)

FIRST VILLAGER (waving a banner). ROUND ONE!

ALL. ROUND ONE!

(ST. GEORGE lowers his spear and rushes at the DRAGON. The crowd is breathless. The DRAGON snorts, roars, squeals and dodges.)

ALL. MISSED! MISSED!

(ST. GEORGE strides back to his place at stage right. He wipes his brow and winks at the BOY.)

ALL. End of Round One!

(The DRAGON gives a ramping exhibit which terrifies the crowd. Then he bows and poses. ST. GEORGE nods that he is ready.)

ALL. Time! ROUND TWO!

(ST. GEORGE *rushes at the* DRAGON, *who leaps from side to side whooping like an Indian.*)

ALL. MISSED! END OF ROUND TWO!

(ST. GEORGE *returns to stage right, sighing heavily. He pats the* BOY *on the shoulder and gives him his spear to hold while the* DRAGON *entertains the crowd with a little dance.*)

ALL. TIME! ROUND THREE!

(ST. GEORGE, *with spear lowered, advances carefully. The* DRAGON *circles. They spar, while the crowd is silent and breathless. Then a quick movement of the* SAINT'S *spear pins the* DRAGON *to the earth.* ST. GEORGE *stands astride the* DRAGON.)

ALL. (*They cheer wildly with great whoops of noise and claps.*) St. George! ST. GEORGE!! ST. GEORGE!!!

FIRST VILLAGER (*above the cheers*). Bain't you going to cut 'is 'ed orf, master?

ST. GEORGE (*commands silence with a gesture*). There's no hurry about that, you know. I have a few words to say first. (*The crowd listens.*) My friends! I have removed your direful scourge. Now I want to ask the Dragon a few questions. Do you, Dragon, see that there are two sides to everything? (*The* DRAGON *nods.*) Are you going to be bad any more? (*The* DRAGON *shakes his head.*) Would you like to stay and settle down here in a peaceful sort of way? (*The* DRAGON *nods vigorously.* ST. GEORGE *draws the spear out of the* DRAGON'S *neck. The* DRAGON *sits up and shakes hands with* ST. GEORGE.) Now, my friends, I do not want you to be prejudiced any more. You are never to go around grumbling and fancying that you have grievances. And you should not be so fond of fights, because next time you might have to do the fighting yourselves, which is not at all the same thing. And now I think we should have some refreshment!

ALL. Refreshment! Celebration! Party! Food! Drink! That's wot we'll have!

(MOTHER *and* FATHER *start passing food and drink to everyone. The crowd starts singing the Tavern song. This time they sing it in four parts, as a round. When everyone has some refreshment ready to eat and drink,* ST. GEORGE *pats the happy* DRAGON *on the head.*)

ST. GEORGE (*lifts his beer mug*). And now I give you—your friend from now on—THE DRAGON!

ALL. OUR FRIEND—THE DRAGON!

(*The* DRAGON *bows courteously as they all drink to him. The* BOY *runs to the* DRAGON *and hugs him, as the* CURTAIN *closes.*)

PRODUCTION NOTES

Because the part of the Dragon was so long and so much fun, we divided it among four actors. They worked out their action very carefully and practiced it together from the first rehearsals. A tall actor was the Head; two middle-sized actors were the Paws, and stood on either side of the Head with an arm around her waist; a smaller actor managed the Tail.

These four actors wore blue tights and blue socks to which claws were attached. (This was an eight-legged dragon.) We covered the Head and Paws with blue cloth which hung just below their knees. Another long piece of the same cloth was attached to their backs and sewn to a wire frame inside of which the Tail actor stood. We cut eye slits at the right places for each actor. The Paw actors wore a blue glove on the hand that showed.

For the other costumes we studied the illustrations by Ernest

H. Shepard in the Holiday House edition of the book. The girls wore long cotton or wool skirts, aprons and blouses, with shawls or scarves over their heads. Bath towels, pieces of burlap and other coarse materials pinned together at the shoulders and tied at the waist with cord made good costumes for the boys. Some of the boys wore hoods or shawls. Some of them fastened rope beards and long hair to their hoods. Some made caps of skin. Several of them, including the Father, hung skins over their shoulders and carried shepherds' crooks. Some actors went barefooted, others wore sandals or sock boots bound with criss-crossed string.

St. George was magnificent in golden armor. His breastplate was made of corrugated cardboard painted gold with a Crusader cross on the front of it. The chain mail of his arms and legs was made from dishcloths sewed together and painted gold. His helmet was made from corrugated cardboard painted gold, with a long plume attached to it. For his first entrance he carried a sword in his belt. At the fight he used a long spear made from a broom handle sharpened to a point and painted gold.

We used our platforms for a big flat stage and left the playing space wide and big for the fight scene. With our blue parachute for the sky we set a cutout wind-blown tree at the back of the stage in the center and a few cutouts of bushes and rocks along the skyline. At one end of the stage we set a two-sectioned hinged screen painted to look like rough boards. This was both the cottage and the Inn. At the other end of the stage we made the entrance to the cave by piling up boxes painted to look like rocks high enough so that the Dragon could stand behind them without being seen by the audience. We twined vines in the rocks and stuck a bush or two in the cracks.

The only stage props we needed were the stools. These were of different heights, so that when the Villagers sat and stood on them they were not all at the same level. We used steps at the front of the stage so that actors could enter from the audience and so that Villagers could stand and sit on them to make the action picture more interesting.

From our netting ceiling we hung cutout paper birds, insects and butterflies strung on black thread.

We used, in addition to our overhead lights, two box floodlights so that we could light either side of the stage when we wished to brighten it, to give the effect of changing scenes, and of time passing.

In working out the action we had actors enter through the audience, singing and talking as they came. This helped keep the play moving as the action changed from one place to another and one day to another.

The song the villagers sang was an old English song which we found on a Vanguard Record, *Tavern Songs of Merrie England*. We also listened to records which used English country speech, so that we could get an idea of how old British shepherd folk sounded. St. George and the Dragon spoke with elegant British accents. The Dragon actors had to speak very loudly, since their faces were not seen.

We used as many Villagers as we needed. There could, of course, be more or fewer. The Dragon could have a different number of actors inside it.

This would be a wonderful play to do outdoors, where the action could be enlarged to have the cave on a hillside where the fight takes place, and the cottage of the Boy separated a bit from the Village Inn. People could come in processions. St. George would be magnificent coming from a distance. And perhaps he could ride a horse. BUT, if the play is done outdoors, figure out how the words can be heard. For, despite the big action scene and the fun of the Dragon action and the fight, this story is full of philosophical conversation which really needs to be heard, or the fun of the story itself is lost.

THE GREAT QUILLOW

THE GREAT QUILLOW

A dramatization based on the story by James Thurber,
published by Harcourt, Brace and Company,
copyright 1944 by James Thurber. Included by
the kind permission of Mr. Thurber.

CHARACTERS

LAMPLIGHTER	BAKER
TOWN CRIER	CANDLEMAKER
TOWN CLERK	COBBLER
BLACKSMITH	CARPENTER
TAILOR	LOCKSMITH
BUTCHER	QUILLOW, the Toymaker
CANDYMAKER	HUNDER, the Giant

*The action of the play takes place in a village square above
which rises a hill. The narrow houses of New Moon Street
have pointed roofs and red chimneys. The only props on stage
are a small bench up center and a street lamp down right, at
the end of the street.*

*The time sequence, which covers several days, will be indi-
cated only by lighting and the music of the bells which we hear
when the clock in the tower strikes the hours.*

*The village clock strikes seven as the curtains open on the
dusk of the village square. After a moment the* LAMPLIGHTER
*enters with his long staff. As he lights the street lamp, the stage
lights creep up a little.*

TOWN CRIER (*circling from rear of audience to front of stage
down right, ringing his bell and chanting*). Town meeting
tonight. Town meeting tonight. Town meeting tonight. . . .

LAMPLIGHTER (*stopping down center stage and turning to*

CRIER). What good is a town meeting when the Giant Hunder sits above our village and curses it. What can we do? He has plundered the villages of the far countryside. And today the earth shook when he strode onto our hillside. He pulled up four trees to make room to sit down!

TOWN CRIER. And when he called to us our doors shook and our windows rattled!

LAMPLIGHTER. What demands has he made?

TOWN CRIER. The Town Clerk has gone to hear Hunder's will. We meet now to hear his demands. (*He continues off down left and around back of audience, his bell ringing softly.*) Town meeting tonight. Town meeting tonight. Town meeting tonight. . . .

(*The* LAMPLIGHTER *stays on stage and is joined now by the line of* VILLAGERS *who follow the* TOWN CLERK *from the rear of the audience onto stage from down right. The* CRIER *has circled the auditorium and has joined the rear of the procession.*)

TOWN CLERK (*as he enters, carrying scroll and quill, and takes his place on the bench up center*). There are 99 other men in the town, but it's the Town Clerk this, and the Town Clerk that, and the Town Clerk everything!

(*The* VILLAGERS, *who are the* TOWN COUNCILORS, *arrange themselves in small groups. They mutter and whisper to each other.* QUILLOW *has followed them in and sits crosslegged on the edge of the stage, down far right.*)

TOWN CLERK. Town meeting will come to order! Town meeting will come to order! (*They quiet down.*) I will now call the roll.

BLACKSMITH. We're all here. You can see that!

TOWN CLERK (*as each name is called the* COUNCILORS *answer impatiently*). Tailor, Butcher, Candymaker, Blacksmith,

Baker, Candlemaker, Lamplighter, Cobbler, Carpenter, Locksmith, Town Crier. (*He looks over his spectacles at* QUILLOW.) We have a visitor tonight, as usual. (*All turn and look amusedly at* QUILLOW.) Quillow, the Toymaker. I will make the proper entry in the minutes.

BLACKSMITH. Never mind the minutes. Read us the demands of Hunder the Giant. (*cries of* Hear! Hear!)

TOWN CLERK (*writing with a flourish*). Quillow, the Toymaker. Now, I will read the minutes of the last meeting.

CANDYMAKER. Let's dispense with the minutes of the last meeting. (*cries of* Hear! Hear!)

TOWN CLERK. It must be properly moved and duly seconded.

TAILOR (*quickly*). I do so properly move.

BUTCHER. And I duly second.

BLACKSMITH. Now read the demands of Hunder the Giant! (*cries of* Hear! Hear!)

TOWN CLERK. Next comes unfinished business. (*all sigh*) We have before us a resolution to regulate the speed of merry-go-rounds. . . .

BLACKSMITH. Dispense with it!

TOWN CLERK. It must be properly moved and duly seconded.

CANDYMAKER. I do so properly move. . . .

BAKER. And I duly second!

TOWN CLERK (*unrolling scroll*). We come now to the business of the day. I have here the demands of Hunder the Giant. The document is most irregular. It does not contain a single "greeting" or "whereas" or "be it known by these presents." (*reads*) "I, Hunder, must have three sheep every morning." (*All:* Three sheep!)

BUTCHER (*aghast*). Why that would use up all the sheep in

the valley in a week and a fortnight, and there would be no mutton for our own people!

TOWN CLERK. "I, Hunder, must have a chocolate a day as high and as wide as a spinning wheel." (*general dismay*)

CANDYMAKER. Why, that would exhaust all the chocolate in my storeroom in three days!

TOWN CLERK. "I, Hunder, must have a new jerkin made for me in a week and a fortnight."

TAILOR (*gasps*). Why, I would have to work night and day to make a jerkin in a week and a fortnight for so large a Giant, and it would use up all the cloth on my shelves and in my basement.

TOWN CLERK. "I, Hunder, must have a new pair of boots within a week and a fortnight."

COBBLER (*moans*). Why, I would have to work night and day to make a pair of boots for so large a Giant in a week and a fortnight, and it would use up all the leather in my workshop and in my back room.

TOWN CLERK. "I, Hunder, must have an apple pie each morning made of a thousand apples."

BAKER. Why, that would use up all the apples and flour and shortening in town in a week and a fortnight; and it would take me night and day to make such a pie, so that I could bake no more pies or cakes or cookies, or blueberry muffins or cinnamon buns or cherry boats or strawberry tarts or plum puddings for the people of the town.

TOWN CLERK. "I, Hunder, must have a house to live in by the time a week and a fortnight have passed."

CARPENTER (*sobs*). Why, I would have to work night and day to build a house for so large a Giant in a week and a fortnight. And all my nephews and uncles and cousins would have to help me, and it would use up all the wood and pegs and hinges and glass in my shop and in the countryside.

LOCKSMITH. I will have to work night and day to make a brass key large enough to fit the keyhole in the front door of the house of so large a Giant. It will use up all the brass in my shop and in the community.

CANDLEMAKER. And I will have to make a candle for his bedside so large it will use up all the wick and tallow in my shop and the world!

TOWN CLERK. This is the final item. "I, Hunder, must be told a tale each day to keep me amused."

QUILLOW (*who has sat all this time with his arms folded and his eyes shut, now opens his eyes and raises his hand*). I will be the teller of tales. I will keep the Giant amused.

CANDYMAKER. Does anyone have any idea of how to destroy the Giant?

(*The* COUNCILORS *think, and then in turn are inspired with a great idea.*)

LAMPLIGHTER. I could creep up on him in the dark and set fire to him with my lighter.

QUILLOW. The fire of your lighter would not harm him any more than a spark struck by a colt-shoe in a meadow.

BLACKSMITH. Quillow is right. But I could build secretly at night an enormous catapult which would cast a gigantic stone and crush Hunder.

QUILLOW. He would catch the stone as a child catches a ball, and he would cast it back at the town and squash all our houses.

TAILOR. I could put needles in his suit.

COBBLER. I could put nails in his boots.

CANDLEMAKER. I could put gunpowder in his candles.

CANDYMAKER. I could put oil in his chocolates.

BUTCHER. I could put stones in his mutton.

BAKER. I could put tacks in his pies.

LOCKSMITH. I could make the handle of his brass key as sharp as a sword.

CARPENTER. I could build the roof of his house insecurely so that it would fall on him.

QUILLOW. The plans you suggest would merely annoy Hunder as the gadfly annoys the horse and the flea annoys the dog.

BLACKSMITH. Perhaps the Great Quillow has a plan of his own. (*all laugh*)

CANDYMAKER. Has the Great Quillow a plan? (*He does not answer.*)

> (*The* COUNCILORS *go out slowly and sadly, muttering about their heavy tasks of the night.* QUILLOW *sits alone thinking. Suddenly his face lightens. He pantomimes the suggestion of the doll he is going to make. He skips off gleefully as the lights dim to off.*
> *The only light on the stage now is that of the street lamp. The town clock strikes five and the* LAMPLIGHTER *enters and puts out the street light, as the stage lights rise for morning.*)

TOWN CRIER (*enters on tiptoe*). Sh! Don't wake the Giant.

LAMPLIGHTER. Sh! His food may not be ready.

TOWN CRIER (*softly*). Five o'clock, and all's well! (*He circles to the rear of the audience. The* VILLAGERS *tiptoe on, wearily carrying their foodstuffs. They line up across the front of the stage, backs to the audience, facing the hill with the sleeping* GIANT.)

BAKER. The pie is baked.

CANDYMAKER. The chocolate is made.

BUTCHER. The sheep are dressed.

LOCKSMITH. I worked all night on the great brass key.

BLACKSMITH. I helped him with my hammer and anvil.

CANDLEMAKER. I have scarcely begun the enormous candle.

CARPENTER. I am weary of sawing and planing.

TAILOR. My fingers are already stiff, and I have just started the Giant's jerkin.

COBBLER. My eyes are tired, and I have hardly begun to make his boots.

TOWN CRIER. Where is Quillow? Where is that foolish little fellow?

LAMPLIGHTER. He was in his shop at midnight, making toys.

ALL. Toys!

LOCKSMITH. He could have helped with the key.

BAKER. The pie.

BUTCHER. The sheep.

COBBLER. The boots.

(QUILLOW *appears smiling and bowing.*)

BLACKSMITH. Well!

QUILLOW. Good morning.

BLACKSMITH. I worked all night with my hammer and anvil helping the locksmith with the great brass key. The Lamplighter tells us YOU spent the night making toys!

QUILLOW (*cheerily*). Making toys, and thinking up a tale to amuse the Giant Hunder.

BLACKSMITH. And a hard night you must have spent hammering out your tale.

LOCKSMITH. And twisting it.

CARPENTER. And leveling it.

BAKER. And rolling it out.

TAILOR. And stitching it up.

COBBLER. And fitting it together.

CANDLEMAKER. And building it around a central thread.

BUTCHER. And dressing it up.

CANDYMAKER. And making it not too bitter and not too sweet.

HUNDER (*awakening, his head and shoulders appear above the hillside, up center*). HO! HO! (*He claps his hands and the* VILLAGERS *fall backwards. He roars with laughter.*) Bring me my sheep, my pie, my chocolate! (*The* VILLAGERS *lug their foodstuffs across the stage, climb on the bench and heave them up to the* GIANT.) Tell me your silly names, and what you do. (HUNDER *gnaws greedily at his food, as the* VILLAGERS *quickly tell their trades, each bowing as he speaks.*)

HUNDER. You! You with the white hair, who are you?

QUILLOW. I am Quillow, the teller of tales.

HUNDER. Bow!

QUILLOW. Wow! (*The others are aghast at his impudence.*)

HUNDER (*scowls with fury, then suddenly laughs*). You are a fairly droll fellow. Perhaps your tales will amuse me. If they do not, I will put you in the palm of my hand and blow you so far it will take men five days to find you. Now, the rest of you, be off to your work. (*The* VILLAGERS *sneak off in terror, as* HUNDER *continues to eat.*) Now, you, tell me a tale.

QUILLOW (*sits cross-legged*). Once upon a time, a Giant came to our town from a thousand leagues away, stepping over the hills and rivers. He was so mighty a Giant that he could stamp upon the ground with his foot and cause the cows in the fields to turn flip-flops in the air and land on their feet again.

HUNDER. Garf! I can stamp upon the ground with my foot and empty a lake of its water.

QUILLOW. I have no doubt of that, O Hunder. But the Giant who came over the hills and rivers many and many a year ago was a lesser Giant than Hunder. He was weak. He fell ill of a curious malady.

HUNDER. Rowf! That Giant was a goose, that Giant was a grass-hopper. Hunder is never sick. (*smites his chest*)

QUILLOW. This other Giant had no ailment of the chest or the stomach or the mouth or the ears or the eyes or the arms or the legs.

HUNDER. Where else can a Giant have an ailment?

QUILLOW (*dreamily*). In the mind, for the mind is a strange and intricate thing. In lesser men than Hunder it is subject to mysterious maladies.

HUNDER. Wumf! Hunder's mind is strong like the rock! (*smites his forehead*)

QUILLOW. No one to this day knows what brought on this dreadful disease in the mind of the other Giant. He suffered no pain. His symptoms were marvelous and dismaying. First he heard the word. For 15 minutes one morning, beginning at a quarter of six, he heard the word.

HUNDER. Harumph! What was the word the Giant heard for 15 minutes one day?

QUILLOW. The word was "woddly." All words were one word to him. All words were "woddly."

HUNDER. All words are different to Hunder. And do you call this a tale you have told me? A blithering goose of a Giant hears a word and you call that a tale to amuse Hunder? I hear all words. This is a good chocolate; otherwise I should put you in the palm of my hand and blow you over the house-tops.

QUILLOW (*as the town clock strikes six*). I shall bring you a better tale tomorrow. No one knows to this day what caused the weird illness in the mind of the other Giant. (HUNDER *growls, yawns, and sinks his great head onto his arms and goes to sleep.* QUILLOW *smiles and goes to downstage right.*)

QUILLOW (*calling softly*). Town Crier! Town Crier! (*The* TOWN CRIER *tiptoes on.*) Call the people. Tell them Quillow has a plan to destroy the Giant Hunder. Call them quietly.

TOWN CRIER (*circling the audience and crying softly*). Town meeting in the village square. Town meeting in . . .

(*As the lights dim into dusk, the* VILLAGERS *enter quietly and form a group around* QUILLOW.)

BLACKSMITH. What is this clown's whim that brings us here like sheep?

(QUILLOW *whispers to the group. They nod and whisper to each other conspiratorially.*)

LAMPLIGHTER. It will never work.

CANDYMAKER. It is worth trying.

TOWN CRIER. I have a better plan. Let all the women and all the children stand in the streets and gaze sorrowfully at the Giant, and perhaps he will go away.

CANDYMAKER. Let us try Quillow's plan. He has a magic, the little man.

(*The lights dim to off. The* VILLAGERS *quietly move to either side of the stage and sit. As the lights rise for morning, the* VILLAGERS *are discovered in their places, with* QUILLOW *sitting cross-legged on the bench below the hillside.*)

HUNDER (*awakening with great noises*). Tell me a tale, small-est of men, and see to it that I do not nod, or I shall put you in the palm of my hand and blow you through yonder cloud.

QUILLOW. Once upon a time, there was a King named Ander-blusdaferafan, and he had three sons named Ufabrodoborobe, Quamdelrodolanderay and Tristolcomofarasee.

HUNDER. Why did this King and his sons have such long and difficult names?

QUILLOW. Ah, it was because of the King's mother, whose name was Isoldasadelofandaloo. One day as the King and his sons were riding through the magical forest, they came upon a woddly. Woddly woddly woddly woddly. Woddly, woddly, woddly. . . .

HUNDER (*bellows*). Say it with words! You say naught but woddly!!

QUILLOW. Woddly woddly woddly woddly. . . .

HUNDER (*roars*). Can this be the malady come upon me? Or do you seek to frighten Hunder?

QUILLOW. Woddly woddly woddly. Woddly woddly woddly.

HUNDER (*in terror, shouts at the* VILLAGERS. *He points to each one as he asks a question and grows more and more horrified as each one answers his question with* Woddly, woddly.) You, Blacksmith, tell me your name? (*to another*) What is the time of day? . . . Where are you going? . . . How are you feeling . . . (*etc.*) All talk! All talk! Say words!

(*The* VILLAGERS *carry on conversations with each other using only the word* Woddly.)

HUNDER (*silencing them with his roaring*). It is the malady! I have heard the word! It is the malady! What am I to do to cure the malady? (*The town clock strikes six.*)

QUILLOW. I was telling you how the King and his three sons rode through the magical forest. . . .

HUNDER. I heard the word. All men said the word.

QUILLOW. What word?

HUNDER. Woddly.

QUILLOW. That is but the first symptom, and it has passed. Look at the chimneys of the town. Are they not red?

HUNDER. Yes, the chimneys are red. Why do you ask if the chimneys are red?

QUILLOW. So long as the chimneys are red, you have no need to worry, for when the second symptom is upon you, the chimneys of the town turn black.

HUNDER. I see only red chimneys, but what could have caused Hunder to hear the word?

QUILLOW (*as the lights dim*). Rest well. I will tell you another tale tomorrow. (*As* HUNDER *goes to sleep,* QUILLOW *signals to the* VILLAGERS. *They quietly move to the chimneys which they pretend to paint. They remove the red cutouts and when they have finished and have returned to their places, the lights come up again for morning.*)

HUNDER (*stirs, rubs eyes, yawns, stretches, and then stares*). The chimneys! The chimneys are black! The malady is upon me again. Teller of tales, tell me what I must do. The chimneys are black! Look, teller of tales, name me fairly the color of yonder chimneys.

QUILLOW. The chimneys are red, O Hunder. The chimneys are red. See how they outdo the red rays of the sun.

HUNDER. The rays of the sun are red, but the chimneys of the town are black.

QUILLOW. You tremble, and your tongue hangs out, and these are indeed the signs of the second symptom. But still there is no real danger, for you do not see the blue men. Or do you see the blue men, O Hunder?

HUNDER. I see the men of the town staring at me. But their faces are white and they wear clothes of many colors. Why do you ask me if I see blue men?

QUILLOW. When you see the blue men, it is the third and last symptom of the malady. If that should happen, you must rush to the sea and bathe in the waters or your strength will become the strength of a kitten. Perhaps if you fast for a day and a night, the peril will pass.

HUNDER. I will do as you say, teller of tales, for you are wise beyond the manner of men. Bring me no food today, tell me no tale. (*He moans and covers his eyes and sleeps.*)

(*The light dims and the* VILLAGERS *softly steal behind the screens so that when the morning light rises there is no one visible except* QUILLOW, *the sleeping* GIANT *and the* TOWN CRIER.)

QUILLOW (*as the town clock strikes five*). Cry the hour. Cry all's well.

TOWN CRIER. Five o'clock! Five o'clock and all's well!

HUNDER (*awakens and looks cautiously at the village*). The chimneys are still black, but I see no blue men. (*grins, smites his chest and roars*) HO, Councilors! Bring me my sheep and my pie and my chocolate, for I have a vast hunger. Behold I am still a whole man! I have heard the word and I have seen the black chimneys, but I have not beheld the blue men.

QUILLOW. That is well, for he who beholds the blue men must bathe in the yellow waters in the middle of the sea, or else he will dwindle first to the height of the pussy willow, then to the height of the daffodil, then to the height of the violet, until finally he becomes a small voice in the grass, lost in the thundering of the crickets.

HUNDER. But I shall remain stronger than the rock and taller than the oak.

QUILLOW. If you are stronger than the rock and taller than the oak, then stamp on the ground and make yonder cow in the field turn a flip-flop.

HUNDER (*gleefully*). Behold, I will make the cow turn twice in the air. (*stamps heavily*)

(*The blue men slide over the village walls and dance up and down in the air.*)

HUNDER (*cries in anguish*). The blue men! The blue men have come! The world is filled with little blue men!

QUILLOW. I see no blue men, but you have begun to shrink like the brook in dry weather, and that is the sign of the third symptom.

HUNDER (*shaking with terror*). The sea! The sea! Point me the sea!

QUILLOW. It is many leagues to the east. Run quickly toward the rising sun and bathe in the yellow waters in the middle of the sea.

(*Bellowing with anguish, HUNDER disappears behind his hillside. As his roaring diminishes the VILLAGERS enter*)

VILLAGERS (*lifting QUILLOW to their shoulders*). THE GREAT QUILLOW!

PRODUCTION NOTES

We made this dramatization of Thurber's tale in six workshop periods. We used our full stage with sections of steps in front of it. We painted two screens to look like New Moon Street in the village. Since we needed to show many chimneys, we painted tall narrow houses on each side of an uphill street. The houses were smaller and smaller as they went up the hill. We painted all of the chimneys black and taped a cutout of red construction paper over each one. Villagers, in dim lighting, easily removed the red papers while they pretended to paint the chimneys black. The other four screens were painted to look like hillside and woods. The six screens were hinged together, so that one corner of the stage was village, the center was hill, and the rest was woods. These screens were set out far enough from the blue-sky back wall for the Villagers to get behind them to work the blue-men trickery, and for Hunder to stand on a stepladder behind the hill screen. He could climb up and down the ladder to increase his height, or to disappear behind the screen. Attached to the back of the top of his screen was a shelf on which he could pile his food. At curtain rise, the Giant was behind the screen, ready to mount his ladder. The Villagers were sitting in the back row of the auditorium. (This is easier and pleasanter for them than backstage, and more interesting for the audience, since such an arrangement lends itself to processions.)

The blue men were cardboard cutouts about 12 inches high, strung on long black threads. These cutouts were placed on the floor behind the screens before the play began. Each thread was carefully curled on top of its own blue man. When the Villagers went behind the screens, each Villager picked up two blue men, and, at the right place in the play, slid the dolls over the tops of the screens and jumped them up and down with the threads. While Quillow and Hunder were rehearsing their scenes, the Villagers made the blue men.

The pie was a big round tray covered with brown-paper crust. The sheep looked like roasted legs of mutton. They were made from big brown paper bags, stuffed and closed at the ends with flutings of paper doilies. The giant chocolate was a stuffed paper bag shaped into a rounded cone to look like a big chocolate drop, painted dark brown, with some twirly drippings.

The Town Clerk carried a long scroll. (*See* page 62.)

The only stage prop was a little stool painted to look like a rock and placed on the stage below Hunder's hill. This is where the Town Clerk sat, and where Quillow sat when he told his stories to Hunder. The other Villagers used the steps in front of the stage to sit on.

The Town Crier carried a bell.

The Lamplighter carried a torch, which he made from a broom handle to which he attached a yellow-paper wick shaded by a little black cardboard shield.

The street light was a floor lamp with a small yellow bulb in the top of it. Over the bulb was a frame, cut out of black cardboard, with yellow gelatin sides. When the Lamplighter touched his lighter to the lamp, he had his back to the audience, so he could actually turn on the lamp while he pretended to light it with his lighter. We twined ivy around the base of the lamp and up the length of it. To make ivy, we cut leaves from green oilcloth and taped them to lengths of thin wire. We used these ivy vines many times. They were most decorative, and we could twine them around stones or windows, along fences, across the edge of the stage, or hang them from our net ceiling. Sometimes we intertwined paper flowers with them.

The lighting of the play not only helped the Villagers to play their tricks, but also took care of the timing of the days. The use of the village clock striking and the Lamplighter lighting and putting out the street lamp, plus the call of the Crier, made the play move from night to day with effectiveness and speed. The clock was a heavy aluminum pan which was hung by its handle off stage, so that it could reverberate when struck with a wooden spoon.

The Doris Lee illustrations in the Harcourt, Brace edition of the book will show you what our costumes looked like. The Villagers wore smocks, pantaloons, long stockings and soft slippers with cardboard buckles. The pantaloons were either pedal pushers, or pajama pants bloused under the knee. Each Villager wore the right kind of hat or apron for his own trade. The Candymaker and the Baker wore white aprons and high white hats; the Blacksmith wore a leather apron; the Tailor safetypinned a pincushion to his apron and had a tape measure sticking out of his apron pocket; the Carpenter, Cobbler and

Locksmith had the tools of their particular trades sticking out of pockets in their leather aprons.

Hunder needed to be costumed only from his waist up. He wore a big stuffed sweat shirt over football shoulder pads. He wore oversized gauntlet gloves. His headpiece was a football helmet covered with a knit shirt to which we sewed masses of rope hair and a great rope beard and attached big rubber Halloween ears. (This same headpiece, in another play, made a good head for a lion.)

If you choose to show all of Hunder, add stuffed knit pajamas belted in at the waist with a very wide oilcloth belt. Strap blocks of wood or tin cans to his feet so that he will be about six inches taller. Over these, he can pull on big hip boots, the kind fishermen wear.

A larger group who made a play from this story added an innkeeper, a minstrel and wives of several of the tradesmen. They started their play with all of the Villagers dancing and singing. The Town Crier rushed in and stopped their gaiety by his news that the Giant Hunder was approaching their happy countryside.

If you wish to have Quillow climb the hill and sit beside the Giant when he tells his tales, put a series of step-up boxes behind the hill screen, so that he can climb up them. He must be very careful not to disturb the blue men when he goes behind the screens.

THE NECKLACE OF PRINCESS FIORIMONDE

THE NECKLACE OF PRINCESS FIORIMONDE

A dramatization based on the story by Mary de Morgan (1880)
found in *Modern Fairy Stories,* edited by R. L. Green,
E. P. Dutton & Co., Inc., New York, 1956

CHARACTERS

PRINCESS FIORIMONDE

YOLANDE,

MELISANDE,

EUNICE, her Ladies-in-waiting

THE KING

THE WITCH

PRINCE PIERROT

PRINCE HILDEBRANDT

PRINCE ADRIAN

PRINCE SIGBERT

PRINCE ALGAR

PRINCE CENRED

PRINCE BALDWYN

PRINCE LEOFRIC

PRINCE RAOUL

PRINCE FLORESTAN

SIR GERVAISE, his Squire

*The scene is the court room of the royal palace, in the days of
magic. The stage is completely open, and the back wall is decorated with royal draperies and coats of arms. At the end of the
stage left, against the back wall, is the couch of the* PRINCESS.
*Below it is the entrance to the royal garden. On the other side
of the stage is an entrance to the rest of the palace.*

When the play opens, the PRINCESS FIORIMONDE *is seated on
the couch. Her* LADIES IN WAITING *are with her.* YOLANDE *sits*

at her feet, strumming a lute. EUNICE *holds a jewel box, out of which hang strings of beautiful jewels.* MELISANDE *holds a golden brush.*

MELISANDE. Let me brush your lovely hair, Princess.

EUNICE. Which jewels will you wear today, Princess?

> (*The* KING *enters from stage right. He walks slowly, in deep thought. The* LADIES IN WAITING *bow deeply. The* PRINCESS *goes to him and curtsies.*)

PRINCESS FIORIMONDE. Why are you sad, my Father?

THE KING. My Daughter, my beautiful Fiorimonde. I am sad that I have no son to rule after my death. It is time we found a suitable Prince for you. Then, when I am too old, he shall be King in my place.

PRINCESS FIORIMONDE. Oh Father, there is plenty of time!

THE KING. No, you are old enough now. Ladies, tell my Heralds to proclaim throughout the country that those of high rank who would pay court to the Princess Fiorimonde will be welcomed. (*He turns and goes off right.*)

LADIES (*bowing*). Yes, your Majesty. (*They follow the* KING *off.*)

> (*The* PRINCESS FIORIMONDE, *left alone, seems to change her character. She frowns and stamps her foot in anger. Then she slowly raises her arms and moves them in a large circle, moving her lips as if speaking to herself. The room grows dark, and there is a noise of thunder. Then the lights are bright again, and the* WITCH *stands beside the* PRINCESS. *The* WITCH *carries a black pot.*)

WITCH (*in a high squeaky voice*). Why do you call me? Why do you disturb me?

PRINCESS FIORIMONDE (*in an unpleasant, complaining voice*). My Father says that I must marry. But YOU know that I

am not really beautiful, but ugly, and that I am not really
good, but wicked. You have made me seem beautiful and
good so that I would not tell my father of you and your
wickedness. And I have never told anyone, and you are safe.
But if I marry, my husband will surely find out that you
visit me. Then you will be killed, and I will lose my beauty.
What can I do so that I need not be married?

WITCH (*puts her pot down, and scratches her head with long
fingernails*). This is truly bad hearing! But we shall beat
them yet! You must deal with each Prince as he comes to
woo you. Would you like them to become dogs, to come at
your call . . . or birds, to fly in the air and sing of your
beauty . . . or would you make them all into beads—the
beads of such a necklace as never woman wore before?

PRINCESS FIORIMONDE (*claps her hands in delight*). The necklace! The necklace! That will be best of all!

WITCH. But this is a dangerous game; for, unless you are very
careful, you yourself may become a bead and hang upon the
necklace with the others!

PRINCESS FIORIMONDE. Nay, never fear. I will be careful. Tell
me what to do.

WITCH (*takes from the pot a golden cord and puts it carefully
over the head of the* PRINCESS, *who now kneels before her*).
Now mind: while this golden cord hangs here, you are safe
enough. But if once you join your fingers around the cord,
you will meet the fate of your lovers, and hang upon the
cord yourself. As for those who would marry you, all you have
to do is to make them close their fingers around the cord. At
once they will be strung upon it as bright, hard beads. There
they shall remain until the cord is cut and they drop off!

(*The room darkens to the sound of thunder.*)

PRINCESS FIORIMONDE (*who is now alone, for the* WITCH *has
vanished, looks down at the cord which hangs around her*

neck). This is really delightful, and I am already quite impatient for the first to come that I may try.

(*The* LADIES IN WAITING *enter and bow.*)

MELISANDE. Dear Princess, the most handsome Prince has come to see you.

EUNICE. His name is Prince Pierrot. And he comes from over the sea, where he rules a large rich country.

MELISANDE. He is truly a proper husband for our beautiful Princess.

THE KING (*enters with Prince Pierrot*). My Daughter, this is the valiant Prince Pierrot, who seeks you for his bride.

PRINCESS FIORIMONDE (*sweetly*). Father, I am quite willing to wed anyone you wish for me.

THE KING. Come, Ladies. We will leave them alone together. (*The* LADIES *follow the* KING *off right.*)

PRINCE PIERROT (*bowing deeply*). Tomorrow, my sweet Princess, you will be my Queen, and share all I possess. What gift would you wish me to give you on our wedding day?

PRINCESS FIORIMONDE. I would have a necklace wrought of the finest gold and jewels to be found. One which is just the length of this gold cord which I wear around my throat.

PRINCE PIERROT (*coming closer to her*). Why do you wear that cord? It has no jewel nor ornament on it.

PRINCESS FIORIMONDE. But there is no cord like mine in all the world. It is as light as a feather, but stronger than an iron chain. Take it in both hands and try to break it, that you may see how strong it is.

(PRINCE PIERROT *pulls at the cord. The lights flash and go out, thunder rolls. When the lights come up,* PRINCE PIERROT *has vanished. On the cord is one bright bead.*)

• 144 •

THE KING (*enters, followed by the* LADIES). Where is Prince Pierrot, my child? I thought he was here talking to you.

PRINCESS FIORIMONDE (*sadly*). He suddenly left me. I am afraid lest I may have given him offense, or perhaps he is ill.

THE KING. Send everyone to find him. We are not pleased that he should treat us in this way. (*The* LADIES *bow and go out.*)

MELISANDE (*running back in*). Your Highness, another suitor has arrived. Prince Hildebrandt is here.

THE KING. Let him come to us.

(EUNICE *and* YOLANDE *enter and announce* PRINCE HILDEBRANDT, *who follows them in.*)

EUNICE. This is Prince Hildebrandt, your Majesty. He comes from a country of the far north of which he will one day be King.

THE KING. Welcome, Prince Hildebrandt. I will leave you with my daughter, while I see what news there is of one who was recently here. (*He goes off right, followed by the* LADIES.)

PRINCE HILDEBRANDT (*kneeling*). Dear Princess, it is indeed great happiness to meet you here on this most beautiful of days. But you are far more beautiful than any day of any year.

PRINCESS FIORIMONDE. And do you not think this bead which I wear on my gold cord is beautiful too?

PRINCE HILDEBRANDT (*rises to look at it*). It is indeed a beautiful bead. Where did it come from?

PRINCESS FIORIMONDE. It came from over the sea, where it shall never return again. Lift the cord from my neck and look at it closely, and tell me if you ever saw one like it.

(PRINCE HILDEBRANDT *starts to lift the cord. Lights. Thunder.*)

PRINCESS FIORIMONDE (*who is now alone, sees that there are two beads on the cord*). Oh, my sweet necklace, how beautiful you are growing! (*She hears the* KING *coming and quickly sits on the couch and hides her face in her hands.*)

THE KING (*enters, with the* LADIES). My Daughter, what is the matter? Where is Prince Hildebrandt?

EUNICE. Why do you weep?

MELISANDE. What has happened to the Prince?

PRINCESS FIORIMONDE (*pretending to weep*). Dear Father, he has left me. Oh, Sire, I pray you will not let people say that when any bridegroom comes to marry me, he flees rather than be my husband. I beg you to summon suitors from far and near that I may not be left alone unwed.

THE KING (*goes to her and caresses her*). My Daughter, what is this plot against us? Both Pierrot and Hildebrandt have disappeared. But there are many more who have come to woo you. Ladies, summon them.

EUNICE. Shall they come in turn, or shall the ones who are now here all be summoned?

THE KING. Have all those who are now here enter that I may speak with them.

> (*The three* LADIES *go to the entrance, stage right, and announce each* SUITOR *in turn. As he is announced, he enters to stage center, bows to the* KING *and to the* PRINCESS, *and then stands against the back wall of the stage. At the end of the introductions, there is a line of* SUITORS *standing at attention across the back of the stage.*)

THE THREE LADIES (*announcing in turn*). Prince Adrian, Prince Sigbert, Prince Algar, Prince Cenred, Prince Baldwyn, Prince Leofric, Prince Raoul!

THE KING (*after each* PRINCE *has been acknowledged and has taken his place in the line-up*). Welcome! You have come to seek the beautiful Fiorimonde as your bride. You may each have a while alone with her, so that she may choose among you to be her husband and my heir. (*He strides across the stage in front of the* PRINCES, *who bow to him as he passes them. As he goes off right, the* LADIES IN WAITING, *who are at that doorway, bow to him.*)

PRINCE ADRIAN (*advances to the* PRINCESS *and kneels to her*). Dear Princess Fiorimonde, you are by far more beautiful than the pictures which I have seen and the stories I have heard. May it please you to let me tell you of my country and the great honor which would be mine if you were my Queen?

PRINCESS FIORIMONDE. Come with me and you shall tell me all about yourself. You others wait here with my Ladies. (*She takes* PRINCE ADRIAN's *hand and leads him off left into the garden.*)

REMAINING PRINCES (*sigh, as they look after her*). She is so lovely!

LADIES. Which will she choose?

(*Lights flicker. Thunder.*)

PRINCESS FIORIMONDE (*enters from the garden. There is a third bead on the cord*). And now who is the next?

PRINCE SIGBERT (*goes to her and kneels*). Dear Princess! Do me the honor of giving me time to woo you. My suit will be brief, but the time to tell you how lovely you are will take the rest of life. (*He rises, gives her his hand, and the two go into the garden.*)

REMAINING PRINCES. She grows even more lovely!

LADIES. It does seem so to us. With each suitor she grows more beautiful!

(*Lights flicker. Thunder.*)

PRINCESS FIORIMONDE (*enters with a fourth bead on the cord*). He was indeed a handsome Prince. But I will hear each of you before I make my choice.

PRINCE ALGAR (*advances and kneels*). Then, dear Princess, I beg that I may be the next to have the privilege and honor of some time alone with you. I have much to say, but my speech is difficult, for your beauty almost makes me silent before you!

PRINCESS FIORIMONDE. A lovely beginning! Do come finish it in the garden. (*They go.*)

REMAINING PRINCES. May I be the one she chooses! (*They look at each other in consternation.*)

LADIES (*laugh*). Remember she can marry only one of you!

(*Lights. Thunder.*)

PRINCESS FIORIMONDE (*enters with a fifth bead on the cord*). And who is next? I can hardly wait!

PRINCE CENRED (*advances and kneels*). Pray, my fairest Princess, let me be the next to talk with you. The whole of my country is preparing for the glorious news they hope I will send them—that you are to be my Queen.

PRINCESS FIORIMONDE. Then come. We don't want your people to be kept too long waiting! (*They go.*)

REMAINING PRINCES. He is too boastful!

LADIES. And you are too nervous!

(*Lights. Thunder.*)

PRINCESS FIORIMONDE (*enters with a sixth bead on the cord*). Only three left! Surely more will come. I want to see many, many, many . . . well, just to be fair, you know.

PRINCE BALDWYN (*advances and kneels*). You are more than fair, you are the fairest! Allow me, dear Princess. (*He rises and takes her hand.*) Perhaps you will not need to see TOO many more after I have talked with you! (*They go.*)

REMAINING PRINCES. Too many more! (*They look at each other.*) TWO more!

LADIES. Two more. Ah, but there have been two and two and two and two. . . .

(*Lights. Thunder.*)

PRINCESS FIORIMONDE (*enters with a seventh bead on the cord*). Only two! But perhaps more will come. I must say I am enjoying myself. Few women will ever know how much!

PRINCE LEOFRIC (*advances and kneels*). Perhaps it is agreeable to you, dear Princess, to be told by so many men of high rank how beautiful and beloved you are. But for us, it is a time of great unease. Pray, keep me waiting no longer! (*He rises, takes her hand, and goes off with her.*)

PRINCE RAOUL. If he is uneasy, then what of me who has been kept waiting longest. But still, there may, I think, be merit in being the last. I will be comforted by that thought.

LADIES. We think she has been very quick to hear these lovely speeches with such speed.

(*Lights. Thunder.*)

PRINCESS FIORIMONDE (*enters with eighth bead on the cord*). And are you the last? It seems a pity. But come!

(PRINCE RAOUL *takes her into the garden. The* LADIES, *left alone, now run over to stage left and look into the garden.*)

EUNICE. Do you not think it strange she seems so joyful?

MELISANDE. There IS something strange about it. She never wanted to get married, you know—not at first!

EUNICE. But she does seem always to grow lovelier.

MELISANDE. There seems something strange about that too!

(*At stage right,* PRINCE FLORESTAN *enters, followed by* GERVAISE.)

GERVAISE. My Prince, I have come with you, but I do not like this. I have heard strange things about suitors who have come to woo this Princess. What happened to Pierrot and to Hildebrandt? I like it not.

PRINCE FLORESTAN. I don't know or care. But this is sure, I have seen her portrait and I will wed her and bring her home as my bride!

GERVAISE. My heart is heavy for you, dear Prince. (*He turns away.*)

(*Lights. Thunder. The* LADIES *scurry back to the entrance at stage right, looking curiously at the new arrivals as they pass them.*)

PRINCESS FIORIMONDE (*enters with a ninth bead on the cord*). Oh another? How nice to have one more!

PRINCE FLORESTAN (*kneels*). Dear Princess, I am Prince Florestan. You are even more beautiful than your portrait which was the most beautiful I ever have seen.

PRINCESS FIORIMONDE. You have my best greetings, Prince Florestan. And you, too, would be my suitor? Come, walk with me and tell me of your home, and all pleasant things. My Ladies, you are dismissed. I think, somehow, he may stay the longest. (*She goes off left with* FLORESTAN.)

(EUNICE *and* MELISANDE *curtsy to her and go off right.* YOLANDE *starts to follow them, but looks back at* GERVAISE.)

YOLANDE. You love your master.

GERVAISE (*turns to her*). Aye, better than anyone else on the earth.

YOLANDE. Then I hope you have said good-by to him, for I fear you will never see him again.

GERVAISE. Why not? And who are you to talk like this?

YOLANDE. My name is Yolande, and I am Princess Fiorimonde's lady. I am the one who is most often in her room with her. And I am fearful. So many suitors have come. And I think none of them will ever be found anywhere again on this earth.

GERVAISE. And where are they gone? And why do you not tell the King, and prevent good men being lost like this?

YOLANDE. Because I fear my mistress. I think she is a sorceress. I have watched her necklace which she wears both day and night. I have watched that necklace growing. First it was only an empty gold cord; then came Prince Pierrot, and when he disappeared the first bead appeared upon the cord. Then came Hildebrandt, and two beads were on the cord instead of one. And now today many suitors have come and now nine beads hang upon the cord, and the tenth will be your own Prince Florestan.

GERVAISE (*starts to draw his sword*). If this be so, I will plunge my sword into Fiorimonde's heart!

YOLANDE. She is a sorceress, and it might be hard to kill her. Besides, that might not break the spell and bring back the men to life. I wish I could show you the necklace, and you might count the beads and see if I do not speak truth. But it is always about her neck, both night and day.

GERVAISE. Take me to her tonight when she is asleep, and let me see it.

YOLANDE. Very well, we will try. But you must be very still. For if she wakes, it will be the worse for both of us.

(Lights. Thunder. YOLANDE *signals* GERVAISE *to leave, and he runs off stage right, as* PRINCESS FIORIMONDE *enters with a tenth bead on her necklace. She is yawning happily.)*

PRINCESS FIORIMONDE. Yolande, it has been a lovely day! How soundly I shall sleep. *(She lies down on the couch. As the lights dim,* YOLANDE *covers the* PRINCESS *with a royal robe.)*

YOLANDE. Good night, Princess. *(She watches her a moment and then goes to the entrance, stage right, and signals.* GERVAISE *tiptoes in.* YOLANDE *whispers.)* She is asleep.

GERVAISE *(softly).* Stay one instant, Yolande. Perhaps, try how I may, I shall fail and either die or become a bead like those who have come before me. But if I succeed and rid the land of your wicked Princess, what will you promise me for a reward?

YOLANDE. What would you have?

GERVAISE. I would have you say you will be my wife, and come back with me to my own land.

YOLANDE. That I will promise gladly. But we must not speak or think of this until we have taken the cord from Fiorimonde's neck. *(She tiptoes over to the sleeping* PRINCESS.*)*

GERVAISE *(follows* YOLANDE *and bends over the* PRINCESS*).* She is so lovely!

YOLANDE. Do not look at her, since her beauty has cost dear already. Look rather at what remains of those who thought her as fair as you do now. See here. *(Bends over and counts the beads.)* And here is a new one! Seek your own master, Prince Florestan, and you will not find him. And you shall never see him again till the charm is broken.

GERVAISE. Of what is the cord made?

YOLANDE. It is of the finest gold. Nay, do not you touch her lest she waken. I will show it to you. (*She puts her fingers around the cord. Lights. Thunder.*)

GERVAISE. Yolande! Yolande! (*He counts the beads.*) Now there is one more bead! Oh, hateful Princess! I know now where go the brave men who came to woo you, and where, too, is my Yolande. (*The* PRINCESS *stirs.* GERVAISE *creeps quickly out of the room, off right.*)

PRINCESS FIORIMONDE (*wakens, as the lights rise*). Why I think, I think . . . did I dream there was someone here? (*She sits up and sees the new bead on her necklace.*) Why there is another bead on my necklace! Who can have come and grasped my chain unknown to me? At any rate, whoever it was is fitly punished. (*laughs*)

(EUNICE *and* MELISANDE *enter from stage right.*)

EUNICE. A new prince has come to be your suitor. And he will not tell his name, but says that he hears that all are bidden to ask for the hand of Princess Fiorimonde, and he, too, would try his fortune.

MELISANDE. He does not look a prince, but is wrapped in a cloak and looks like a peasant.

PRINCESS FIORIMONDE (*rises and stretches pleasantly*). Let him come at once. Be he prince or peasant, what care I? (*The* LADIES *go out.* GERVAISE *enters, wrapped in a long cloak.*) You are most welcome, stranger. What have you heard of me?

GERVAISE. I have heard that you are the most beautiful woman in the world.

PRINCESS FIORIMONDE. And is that true?

GERVAISE. No, Princess, that is not true. You are very beautiful, but I have seen a woman who is fairer.

PRINCESS FIORIMONDE (*angrily*). Who is she? Where is she? Bring her here at once that I may see if you speak truth.

GERVAISE. What will you give me to bring her to you? Give me that necklace you wear, and I will summon her in an instant.

PRINCESS FIORIMONDE (*disturbed*). You have asked for the only thing from which I cannot part.

GERVAISE. You can see her for the necklace, but for nothing else.

PRINCESS FIORIMONDE. Well . . . take it off my neck then.

GERVAISE. No, indeed not. I am no servant and should not know how to unclasp it. I shall return, my Lady. Think it over. (*He goes off left.*)

(PRINCESS FIORIMONDE *watches him go. She frowns and bites her lip. Then she raises her arms and waves them. The lights flash, thunder roars, and the* WITCH *is there.*)

WITCH. You called me, my dear? How goes the necklace? Right merrily, I see. Eleven beads already! (*She looks more closely.*) But what is that one? It is different from the others.

PRINCESS FIORIMONDE. That is one thing I want YOU to tell me. Last night when I slept there were ten beads. This morning there are eleven. I know not from whence comes the last.

WITCH. It is no suitor, but some young maid.

PRINCESS FIORIMONDE. It must be Yolande! She was not with my Ladies this morning. She tried to rob me of my necklace as I slept! Well, she is punished now, and so may be all others who would do the same!

WITCH. And when will you get the twelfth bead?

PRINCESS FIORIMONDE. He waits at the palace now. And this is why I summoned you. He would not touch the necklace. And he said that he knew a woman fairer than I!

WITCH. Why should you heed tales of other women fairer than you? You know that I have made you the most beautiful woman in the world. This is some trick! Beware, Princess, beware! Give no ear to what this stranger says, or you shall rue it!

PRINCESS FIORIMONDE. I do not like to hear anyone speak of another as beautiful as I!

WITCH. Are you so silly and vain as to be troubled because a man says what you know is false? Be warned in time! I tell you, do not listen to him; but get him on your chain so he will speak no more! (*the lights flash, thunder rolls, and as the* WITCH *disappears, she wails*) Get . . . him . . . on . . . your . . . chain!

> (*The* PRINCESS FIORIMONDE *paces back and forth in deep thought. Then she goes to stage right and looks out. She sees* GERVAISE *and beckons to him.*)

PRINCESS FIORIMONDE (*sweetly*). Dear Sir, I have been thinking. I think that you were jesting when you said you knew a woman fairer than I.

GERVAISE (*standing at stage right*). Doubtless you are very beautiful. So why should you mind my telling you that I have seen a woman lovelier?

PRINCESS FIORIMONDE. You say you will bring her to me, if I give you my necklace. This is because you want my beads because there are none so beautiful in all the world as these jewels on my chain.

GERVAISE (*walks in front of her and dangles a necklace of acorns from his wrist*). I have a necklace here which pleases me better.

PRINCESS FIORIMONDE. What is that necklace? Where did you get it?

GERVAISE (*pleasantly*). I like my necklace better than yours,

Princess. And, believe me, there is no necklace like mine in all the world.

PRINCESS FIORIMONDE (*furiously*). Why? Is it a fairy necklace? What does it do? Pray give it to me! Was it worn by the woman you thought more beautiful than I? Is that why she seemed so fair? Give it to me!

GERVAISE (*holding his acorn chain away from her grasping hands*). Come, I will make a fair exchange. Give me your necklace and you shall have mine. And when mine is round your throat, I will say that you are the fairest woman in the world!

PRINCESS FIORIMONDE. Take mine then! (*In an eager rage to get the acorn chain, she tears at the one which is around her own neck. The lights flash, thunder rolls, the necklace which she has broken falls on the floor. When the lights come up, the PRINCESS has vanished.*)

GERVAISE (*bending over the necklace and counting*). Twelve! O clever Princess! You are not so very clever, I think, to be outwitted!

THE KING (*enters from stage right, followed by MELISANDE and EUNICE*). I thought I heard my Daughter's voice. Where is the Princess Fiorimonde?

GERVAISE (*bows to the KING*). A moment ago she was here with me. Now let me see if I cannot bring her to you. But first, let me bring those who have been longer lost than she! (*With his sword, he points to the necklace on the floor*) Now, let us first find the valiant Prince Pierrot! (*With his sword, he cuts off the first bead. The lights go out, thunder rolls.*)

PRINCE PIERROT (*now standing on the stage, his arm raised in fury*). Treachery! The wicked Princess Fiorimonde!

THE KING AND LADIES (*amazed*). Prince Pierrot!

(GERVAISE *cuts off another bead, and another. The action is repeated for each suitor, until each one has returned. After they are all there,* GERVAISE *raises his sword once again.*)

GERVAISE. And now, here is she who has helped to save you all!

(*This time, it is* YOLANDE *who appears.* GERVAISE *goes to her, kneels, and kisses her hand.*)

THE KING (*in deep sorrow*). We owe you deep amends, O noble Princes and fair Yolande! Surely our Daughter has been under some fearful spell of black magic. What punishment do you wish us to prepare for her?

GERVAISE. Give her no other punishment than that she be what she really is—a plain and lonely woman. For her power now is gone. Whatever evil spirit has had her under a spell will vanish now forever. (*He goes to the necklace and cuts off the last bead.*)

(*As the lights flash, above the roll of thunder comes a piercing cry, as the* WITCH *screams in agony. When the lights come up,* PRINCESS FIORIMONDE, *her face covered with a veil, kneels sadly before her Father.*)

PRODUCTION NOTES

"We want to do a scary play!"

"One full of bad magic!"

"But not a fairy story everyone knows. Something the audience never heard of!"

So we decided to try *The Necklace of Princess Fiorimonde*, although it was longer than most of our plays and had hard problems to solve.

How did we turn the actors into beads on a necklace? We strung twelve beads on a long gold ribbon, tied the ribbon ends together, and bunched all the beads closely together on one part of the ribbon. The ribbon was wide enough, so that the beads would not slip unless they were pulled. When the Witch took this necklace out of her pot, she kept the bunched beads hidden in one hand, as she put the ribbon over Fiorimonde's head. She tucked the beads under Fiorimonde's shoulder cape, so the audience saw only the gold ribbon hanging down in front. From the earliest rehearsals, we used this necklace and the little cape, so our magic would be sure to work properly. We planned the play so that each time an actor was to vanish he was at the edge of the stage when he took hold of the necklace. Then he could quickly step off stage while the lights were out. (Actually most of the vanishings happened in the garden, which was off stage where there was no problem.) Each time the lights went out, the Princess quickly pulled one bead from under the cape, along the ribbon, to the front of her necklace. Before she herself turned into a bead, she slipped the necklace off and dropped it on the floor, while the lights were out. Gervaise picked it up with the tip of his sword so that the audience really saw it before he cut off the beads. But when he put it back on the floor, he placed it behind a flower border at the front of the stage, where the audience could not see it. The action and sound of cutting and the convincing expressions of the actors made the audience believe that the beads were really being cut off each time. The necklace, of course, was never seen by the audience again.

The worker of the lights was a most important person to this play, because the lights had to go off and on at exactly the right times. He also had to shake the piece of tin which hung beside him for the thunder.

What happened to the suitors who disappeared? They had to have a place off stage where, during the actual performance, they could sit quietly and be ready to reappear instantly. We made a high hedge at the garden end of the stage and put benches behind it so the off-stage actors could sit there. We made four frames of 1-inch-by-2-inch wood strips and attached to them a long high piece of chicken wire covered with canvas painted dark green. We did not attach the frames to each other, but left spaces between them so that the hedge would curve. We braced each frame with an 18-inch strip of wood, so the hedge would stand by itself.

The stage area had to be open for the large-action scenes. We used our screens across the back of the stage and hung royal draperies on them. A bench covered with a velvet drape was the Princess's couch. Behind it we used our window screen richly draped.

A section of steps at the right end of the stage was the entrance from the rest of the palace; another section of steps at the left end led to the garden. We put a border of flowers across the front of the stage. We found that flower borders were useful to decorate many of our plays. We made them of strips of beaverboard braced with wood to make them stand. Cut out at the top and painted like flowers, shrubs and grass, they were most effective.

All the royal and rich materials and costumes from everyone's attic were used in this play. The Princess and her Ladies wore flowing skirts, draped sleeves, pointed hats with veils. Some of the Princes wore tights, tunics and shoulder capes. Others wore long robes. All wore fancy belts and jewels.

The Witch had a big loose purple robe, on which she painted magic designs with florescent paint. She made a peaked cardboard hat with a brim, and painted snakes on it. To it she sewed long straggly hair made of green yarn.

Gervaise carried the sword which we had made for *Arthur's Sword*. (*See* page 43.) Other Princes who wished to have swords made theirs to suit their own tastes.

There were many different crowns in this play. Some actors made theirs of narrow paper bands. Others made wide ones cut into peaks or scallops or curves. A few made theirs of tin. They covered their crowns with foil, or painted them, pasted bits of colored beads or shiny foil on them for jewels, glued glitter to them for designs or edgings. Corrugated paper makes good crowns, because it curves nicely, looks heavy, and is very durable.

In many of our plays all the actors are on stage most of the time. In this play, however, there are times when only a few actors are on stage. In rehearsals, Fiorimonde, the Witch, Gervaise and Yolande could work on these smaller scenes by themselves, while the larger scenes were being rehearsed on the stage.

Since Yolande's part was a long one, she was given no lines until her meeting with Gervaise. She was a part of the action, but the other two Ladies had all the dialogue.

Each suitor tried to make his character different from the others. They had fun practicing formal entrances, walks and bows. When they were not rehearsing their scenes, they were busy helping work out the lighting, sound effects, scenery, props and costume problems.

You can change the number of actors in this play by adding or subtracting suitors and Ladies in Waiting. Girls make as good Princes and Kings as boys do.

STORY SUGGESTIONS

There are many stories that are good to dramatize. These are some of them.

Fairy Tales

Cinderella
The Emperor's New Clothes
The Golden Goose
Hansel and Gretel
Rumpelstiltskin
The Sleeping Beauty
The Snow Queen
Snow White
The Twelve Dancing Princesses

Folk Tales

The Conjure Wives
The Raggle-Taggle Gypsies
The Stone in the Road
The Wise Men of Gotham

Bible Stories

The Good Samaritan
Joseph and His Brothers

Myths

King Midas and the Golden Touch
Pandora's Box
Thor's Quest of the Hammer

Stories from Shakespeare

Julius Caesar
Macbeth
The Merchant of Venice
Midsummer Night's Dream
The Taming of the Shrew
The Tempest

Hero Tales and Legends

Arabian Nights stories
Aucassin and Nicolette
Hercules
Joan of Arc
King Arthur
Marco Polo
Robin Hood
Tyll Eulenspiegel
Ulysses
William Tell

Favorite Stories Old and New

Alice in Wonderland—Lewis Carroll
Amahl and the Night Visitors—Gian-Carlo Menotti
The Bean Boy—Monica Shannon
The Bojabi Tree—Edith Rickert
A Christmas Carol—Charles Dickens
Elsie Piddock Skips in her Sleep—Eleanor Farjeon
Ferdinand—Munro Leaf
The Five Hundred Hats of Bartholomew Cubbins—Dr. Suess
The Happy Prince—Oscar Wilde
The House at Pooh Corner—A. A. Milne
Huckleberry Finn—Mark Twain
In the Great Walled Country—Raymond MacDonald Alden
Just So Stories—Rudyard Kipling
The Knights of the Silver Shield—Raymond MacDonald Alden
The Lady or the Tiger—Francis Richard Stockton
The Little Dressmaker—Eleanor Farjeon
Madeline—Ludwig Bemelmans
Many Moons—James Thurber
Mary Poppins—Pamela Travers
Mary Poppins Comes Back—Pamela Travers
Mary Poppins in the Park—Pamela Travers
Mary Poppins Opens the Door—Pamela Travers
The Nürnberg Stove—Louise de la Ramé
Peter Pan—James M. Barrie
The Pied Piper of Hamelin—Robert Browning
Rip Van Winkle—Washington Irving
Tales of the Alhambra—Washington Irving
The Thirteen Clocks—James Thurber

Tom Sawyer—Mark Twain
Treasure Island—Robert Louis Stevenson
Twig—Elizabeth Orton Jones
The Wind in the Willows—Kenneth Grahame
Winnie the Pooh—A. A. Milne
The Wizard of Oz—L. Frank Baum

READY-MADE PLAYS

There are many good ready-made plays, and these are some of them. You have to ask permission from the publisher to produce these plays. He will tell you if you must pay a royalty fee.

The Bellman of Mons by Dorothy Rose Coogins. In *The Atlantic Book of Junior Plays*, Little, Brown & Co., Boston
A charming medieval play for fourteen actors, with extras.

Columbine Madonna by Glenn Hughes. In *The Appleton Book of Holiday Plays*, D. Appleton & Co., New York
A beautiful Christmas fantasy for five girls.

The Gooseberry Mandarin by Grace Dorcas Ruthenburg. In *Plays of American Life and Fantasy*, Coward-McCann, Inc., New York
A tiny play of fun and beauty in the Chinese manner for four characters. Good for outdoor performing.

The Invisible Duke by F. Sladen-Smith. In *One-Act Plays of To-Day, Fifth Series*, J. W. Marriott, ed., George G. Harrap & Co., Ltd., London
Magic and melodrama for six characters.

Jephtha's Daughter by Elma Ehrlich Levinger. Samuel French, Inc., New York
Also in *The Atlantic Book of Junior Plays*.
A lovely dramatization based on the story in Judges XI, with eleven speaking parts and extras. For older actors.

Kinfolk of Robin Hood by Percy Mackaye. In *The Atlantic Book of Junior Plays*, Little, Brown & Co., Boston
A long, exciting play in four scenes for twenty players and more (or less). Full of fun, suspense and beauty.

The Knave of Hearts by Louise Saunders. Longmans, Green & Co., Inc., New York
Fun for Valentine's Day in the kitchen of the King. Ten characters and extras.

The Land of Heart's Desire by William Butler Yeats. The Macmillan Co., New York
A beautiful but difficult Irish fantasy for six characters.

A Little Child by Jessie Orton Jones. The Viking Press, Inc., New York

A Christmas Pageant for many small actors.

The Lost Princess by Dan Totheroh. Samuel French, Inc., New York
Exciting Chinese fun for fifteen actors, with extras. A sequel to *The Stolen Prince* (see below).

The Maker of Dreams by Oliphant Down. Walter H. Baker Co., Boston

One of the nicest Pierrot-Pierrette plays for three characters.

Miracle Plays by Anne Malcolmson. Houghton Mifflin Co., Boston
A book of seven medieval plays beautifully adapted for young moderns.

The Pie and the Tart by Mathurin Dodo. In *The Appleton Book of Holiday Plays,* D. Appleton & Co., New York
An adaptation of a 15th-century French farce for four actors.

Pink and Patches by Margaret Bland. Samuel French, Inc., New York
A southern mountain play for three girls and one boy. Especially good for outdoors.

The Play of St. George by J. M. C. Crum. In *The Atlantic Book of Junior Plays,* Little, Brown & Co., Boston
As many actors as you want to use can have fun with this spoof of St. George and the Dragon.

The Prince Who Was a Piper by Harold Brighouse. Samuel French, Inc., New York
A humorous poetic play for thirteen older actors, plus extras.

Rehearsal by Christopher Morley. Longmans, Green & Co., Inc., New York
A very simple play for six girls. No costumes or staging.

Six Who Pass While the Lentils Boil by Stuart Walker, Samuel French, Inc., New York
Also in *Portmanteau Plays,* D. Appleton & Co., New York
Fun indoors or out. Large cast with good parts for all.

Sir David Wears a Crown. A sequel to the above with the same characters plus several new ones. Samuel French, Inc., New York
In *Portmanteau Adaptations* by Stuart Walker, D. Appleton & Co., New York

Spreading the News by Lady Gregory. Samuel French, Inc., New York
An Irish farce for ten characters. Simple setting. Very good outdoors.

The Stolen Prince by Dan Totheroh. Samuel French, Inc., New York
A sequel to *The Lost Princess* (above), but with some exciting bandits added. Fifteen characters and extras.

Ten Minutes by the Clock by Alice C. D. Riley. Walter H. Baker Co.,
  Boston
  Fun at the royal breakfast table. Nine characters.
Three Pills in a Bottle by Rachel Field. Samuel French, Inc., New York
  In *Plays of the 47 Workshop I*, Brentanos, New York
  Fantasy for eight characters.

SOME HELPFUL BOOKS

Berk, Barbara and Bendick, Jeanne, *How to Have a Show*. Franklin Watts, Inc., New York, 1957

Berk, Barbara and Bendick, Jeanne, *The First Book of Stage Costume and Make-up*. Franklin Watts, Inc., New York, 1954

Burger, Isabel B., *Creative Play Acting*. A. S. Barnes & Co., New York, 1950

Lease, Ruth Gonser and Siks, Geraldine Brain, *Creative Dramatics in Home, School and Community*. Harper & Brothers, New York, 1952

Leeming, Joseph, *The Costume Book*. J. B. Lippincott Co., Philadelphia, 1938

Siks, Geraldine Brain, *Creative Dramatics*. Harper & Brothers, New York, 1958

Ward, Winifred, *Creative Dramatics*. D. Appleton-Century Co., Inc., New York, 1930

Ward, Winifred, *Playmaking with Children*. Appleton-Century-Crofts, Inc., New York, 1947

Ward, Winifred, *Stories to Dramatize*. Children's Theatre Press, Anchorage, Kentucky, 1952

Ward, Winifred, *Theatre for Children*. D. Appleton-Century Co., Inc., New York, 1939

Damaged note 4 / 2 / 16
Pg. 141 torn. Repaired with booktape. KDQ